the music of
FRANK BRIDGE

ANTHONY PAYNE
LEWIS FOREMAN
JOHN BISHOP

Thames Publishing
14 Barlby Road, London W10 6AR

This edition of 'The Music of Frank Bridge'
first published 1976 by Thames Publishing
in conjunction with the Royal College of Music
Frank Bridge Trust

Printed by *John G Eccles Printers Ltd, Inverness*

ISBN 0 905210 02 6

This book is sold subject to the condition that it shall not, by way of trade or otherwise, be lent, resold, hired out or otherwise circulated without the publisher's prior consent, in any form of binding or cover other than that in which it is published and without a similar condition, including this condition, being imposed on the subsequent purchaser. The contents, or any part of them, may not be reproduced without permission from the publishers.

© 1976 Anthony Payne   Lewis Foreman   John Bishop

CONTENTS

	Page
Introduction (John Bishop)	5
Bridge — the man	5
The music (Anthony Payne)	9
The early years	9
The middle period	21
Years of transition	27
The final harvest	32
Illustrations	52
Catalogue of works (Lewis Foreman)	55
Introduction	55
Original works	58
Arrangements	78
Works by category	78
Bibliography (John Bishop)	81
Discography (John Bishop)	84
Index	87

Music examples are reproduced by kind permission of Boosey and Hawkes Ltd, Stainer and Bell Ltd, and Faber Music Ltd.

Photographs were kindly loaned by Benjamin Britten, Florence Hooton, Daphne Oliver, Brenda Little and John Alston.

INTRODUCTION

JOHN BISHOP

1976 is a particularly happy moment to launch this book, for a spate of new gramophone records, representing most sides of Bridge's art (see page 84), will bring his music before a much wider public than hitherto. Their issue marks a growing interest in Bridge which this book, and other ventures initiated by the RCM Frank Bridge Trust, will — hopefully — intensify. Anthony Payne's analysis of the music is an expansion of an article that appeared in two issues of *Tempo* (to the editor of which we acknowledge our thanks). Lewis Foreman's compilation is the first published complete list of works, although mention must be made of the longhand list prepared for the Parry Room, Royal College of Music, by Oliver Davies; the largest single collection of Bridge manuscripts is kept in the Parry Room.

The RCM Frank Bridge Trust was set up after Mrs Bridge's death, in 1961. As well as its activities sponsoring recordings and publications, small grants are given to reputable concert-giving bodies and artists who include Bridge's larger works in their programmes. All enquiries should be sent to the Bursar at the RCM, Prince Consort Road, London SW7.

Bridge — the man

It is certainly ironic — though not untypical of English musical life — that Frank Bridge (1879-1941) is known to the concert-going public only as the source of a theme on which his pupil Benjamin Britten wrote a dazzlingly effective set of variations for strings. Beginner pianists encounter Bridge in pieces like *Rosemary* or the *Three sketches,* and those few remaining art-song singers occasionally give *Love went a-riding* an airing. But for the rest, almost total neglect, with the exception of the light orchestral pieces like *Cherry Ripe.* There is as yet no society devoted to keeping his works before the public, as there is for Elgar, Delius, Warlock and others, and comparatively little has been written about him (see page 81). Peter J. Pirie's is the only book before this one. Benjamin Britten and Peter Pears have, of course, many times included Bridge works in their recital and orchestral programmes — Britten's performance on record with Rostropovich of the cello sonata is superb — but few other musicians currently carry conviction to the point of seeing that Bridge features in their repertoire. The BBC have been an honourable exception, broadcasting many of the later works, including *Phantasm, Oration* and *Rebus*.

Bridge was steeped in music from his earliest years. His father conducted a theatre orchestra in Brighton, in which young Frank played violin; he filled in for missing instrumentalists and also made arrangements — a sure proving ground for a musician who was nothing if not utterly practical.

He entered the RCM in London as a violin student, won a composition scholarship in 1899 and studied for four years with Stanford. On leaving college he was at first a professional violinist but later switched to the viola, with the English String Quartet and other groups. One reads of him, for example, taking part with the ESQ in a performance (1913) of Ravel's *Introduction and Allegro* with the composer conducting (*sic*), and the following year in a performance of one of Fauré's piano quartets, with the composer as pianist.

Bridge began to make a name for himself in the pre-1914 period as a composer and as a reliable conductor, both in the concert hall and opera house, including Covent Garden. Sir Henry Wood turned to him as a deputy on a number of occasions. As Herbert Howells put it: 'Bridge, more than any man in recent musical history, could survive with dignity, and even with profit, the ordeal of conductor-as-proxy, and leave his compatriots wondering why it was so often necessary for a celebrity's toothache to be the ridiculously inadequate excuse for our having the opportunity to hear a naturally endowed native conductor'.

Bridge continued to conduct after the war, and went in 1923 to the United States, to conduct his own compositions with leading American orchestras. The American patroness of music Mrs Elizabeth Coolidge became a friend, and was the dedicatee of several works.

He also continued conducting in England. The programme he directed for a Royal Philharmonic Society concert in 1929 was, for example, Mozart's *Magic Flute* overture, the Delius violin concerto, Bax's *In the faery hills*, excerpts from Rimsky-Korsakov's *Coq d'Or*, and Brahms's Second Symphony. Two years previously the young Benjamin Britten had been 'knocked sideways' when he heard Bridge conduct *Enter Spring* at the Norwich Triennial Festival.

Not too much is known about Bridge the man, but what *is* known is revealing. Britten, writing of his first meeting and composition lessons with Bridge, has said: 'We got on splendidly . . . I used to go regularly to him, staying with him in Eastbourne or in London, in the holidays from my prep school . . . I badly needed his kind of strictness; it was just the right treatment for me. His loathing of all sloppiness and amateurishness set me standards to aim for that I have never forgotten . . . Bridge insisted on the absolutely clear relationship of what was in my mind to what was on the paper. I used to get sent to the other side of the room. Bridge would play what I had written and demand if it was what I really meant'.

Writing of the Bridges' home, Britten said: 'It was, of course, the first time I had seen how an artist lived. I heard conversation which centred around the arts; I heard the latest poems discussed, and the latest trends in painting and sculpture. He also drove me round the south of England and opened my eyes to the beauty of the Downs and the magnificence of English ecclesiastical architecture . . . In everything he did for me there were, perhaps above all, two cardinal principles. One was that you should try to find yourself and be true to what you found. The other — obviously connected with it — was his scrupulous attention to good technique, the business of saying clearly what was in one's mind. He gave me a sense of technical ambition'.

Sir Arthur Bliss recalls an occasion when he sat with Bridge on a panel judging entries for a composition competition. As score after score was passed to him, Bridge immediately turned to the last two or three pages: 'He affirmed', says Bliss, 'that the ending would give a very fair inkling of a composer's individuality — no need at once to plough through the whole work!'

And Eric Coates gives another indication of Bridge's concern with practicalities. Talking about orchestration he said: 'Eric, don't double more than you can help'. Coates pays tribute to Bridge in this way: 'What a nice fellow he was, sympathetic, kind, helpful, understanding, an artist to his fingertips and generous in his praise of others'.

Bridge, naturally an ebullient, resilient man, was often as frank as his name — honest, blunt, and impatient with the shortcomings of others. He chose not to wrap his pills in sugar yet had, as a friend of long standing asserted in a memorial tribute, 'a heart of gold and a sense of loyalty in friendship that is very rare'.

Pianist Angus Morrison speaks of an occasion when Bridge took him, Jean Pougnet and Anthony Pini through the Trio No 2, explaining exactly how he wanted it played: 'He coached us and what he taught us about one particular phase or nuance was like all the instruction of a fine musician: it applied to so much else in music, too. Bridge was one of the most highly professional musicians I have known — and professional in the best sense. I don't mean slick, I mean with a tremendous sense of integrity and understanding of the art of music'.

That he got fine results from the professionals we know, but he was also successful with the amateur Audrey Chapman (Melville) Orchestra, which he trained for many years and which achieved high standards.

Bridge met his wife Ethel, an Australian, as a fellow student in the second violins of the RCM Orchestra; there was, by all accounts, a beautiful companionship. Bridge was very domesticated and a colleague recalls how efficiently he coped with all the catering on a musicians' holiday.

Bridge was very much a Sussex man and in the 1920s had built for him a small country house on top of the downs at Friston, near Eastbourne; all his later works were written there. Peter Pears recalls how enormously enjoyable were visits: Bridge lived, he says, a 'straightforward, simple but lively and warm sort of existence' there for the rest of his life.

But besides being eminently practical he was not without a sense of fun. There is a touching account of his role as inspiration of the 'Chips Quartet', which used to entertain the annual parties of the RCM Union with musical snippets arranged for unlikely combinations — *Sweet and Low* on four double-basses was an example.

After the First World War he wrote some left-hand-only piano pieces for Douglas Fox, to whom he commented charactistically: 'I doubt whether you will be attracted when you try these pieces through at first, but just work a little at them and then I fondly hope they will stand up on their own legs and smile at you'.

Britten's debt to Bridge extended well beyond the development of his compositional craft. They discussed everything, including pacifism, which in Bridge's case was 'not aggressive, typically gentle'. One of the few ways Britten could repay Bridge was with the latter's tennis, which was, said Britten, 'wild and unconventional'.

Bridge died in 1941, when the nation's interests were elsewhere than music. For the last ten years he had steadily slid out of the public consciousness, yet was working away at his important last works and was, one feels, at the height of his powers when the end came.

He has certainly not had his due, and in acknowledging this we can perhaps relish the thought that the discoveries are there for us to make.

Drawings by Marjorie Fass of Bridge conducting a BBC orchestra on January 21, 1935.

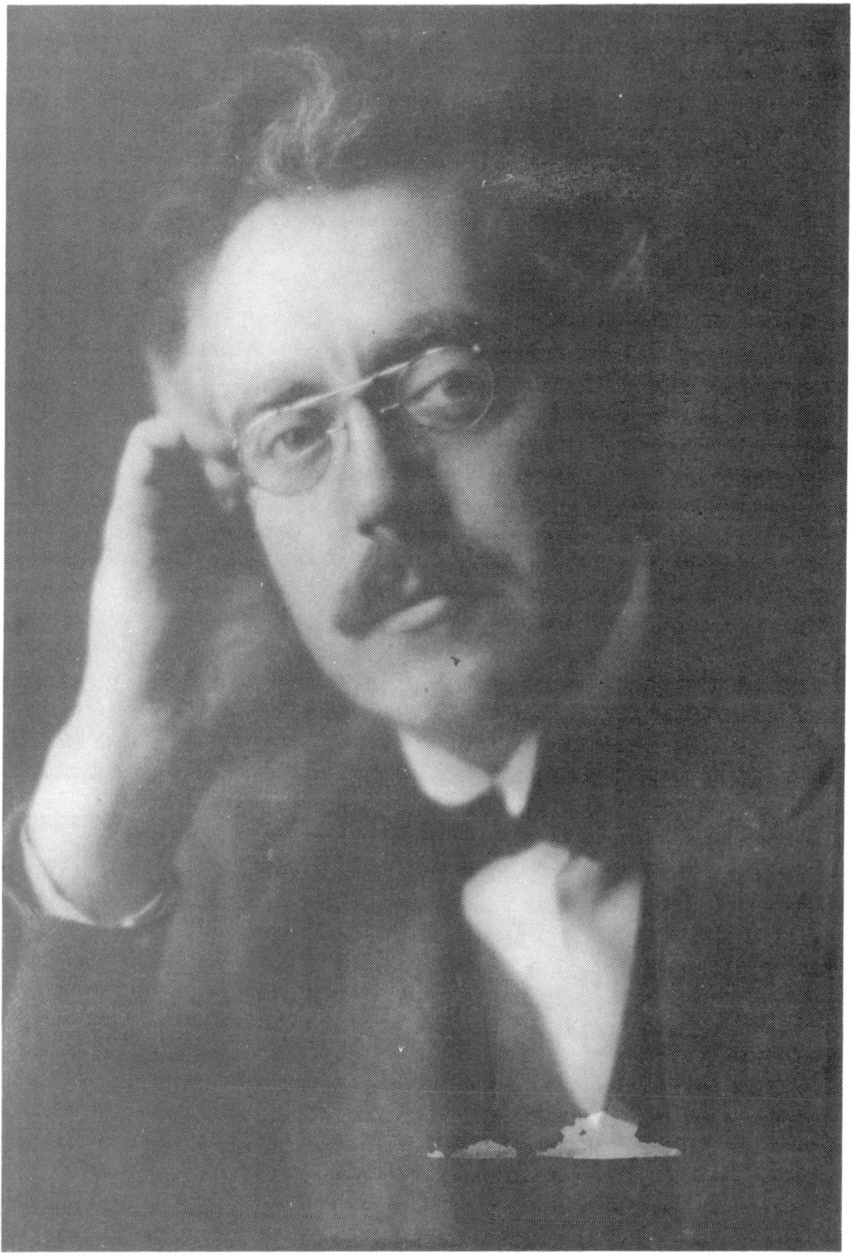

THE MUSIC

ANTHONY PAYNE

The early years

The neglect of Frank Bridge's music by performers and writers since his untimely death in 1941 has delayed a full examination of one of the most fascinating developments of style and personality in 20th-century English music. It is the record of an artist's slow recognition of his deepest self, after a leisurely decade of reasoned creative work in which he does not seem to have felt the need to explore the deeper recesses of his personality, or more probably found it impossible to face such dark sources of inspiration and revelation, and temporarily suppressed them. It was only after a long period of emotional and intellectual development that his rich and complex character proved capable of revealing itself, enabling Bridge to balance his rational and orderly flow of ideas with a dark, irrational fantasy. Possibly the experience of the war marshalled the hidden forces in Bridge's nature, and forced him to come to terms with them. But even without such a catalyst his enquiring mind, always alert to the development of style and language, might have led him on to self-discovery by means of technique. Certainly the music prior to his unexpectedly radical development in the 1920s is of slowly increasing depth and individuality.

From the outset of his career Bridge had possessed an exceptionally fluent and logically ordered technique which stemmed from 19th-century German methods and was tempered by a Gallic clarity and lightness. Unlike his many British contemporaries who had received a similar German-based grounding in composition, he does not seem to have questioned its premises. No antidote was required to their manner of thematic argument, functional harmony and tonal architecture, as it was in the case of Holst, Vaughan Williams, Ireland and others. This factor accounts for the difference between his music and that of, say, Bax and Ireland, with whom he shared (at least until the middle 1920s) more than a few turns of phrase and harmony. The vocabulary might have been similar, but hardly the syntax. This cast of thought enabled him later to assimilate elements of Bergian expressionism, and alienated him from a public more used to British composers whose modernism was tinged with Debussy, Ravel or Stravinsky.

If Bridge's Germanic predilections arose from the Brahmsian training of his teacher Stanford, his early language is certainly not slavishly imitative. It rarely sounds like Brahms, and a personal identity, although as yet pale in outline, is nearly always evident. In the touching innocence of its romanticism there is no trace of foreboding, no premonition that the innocence will one day be destroyed. Texturally the composer it most often calls to mind is Fauré — the Fauré of the Piano Quartets and Violin Sonata, where the vestiges of a Brahmsian influence are likewise being dissolved. There is the same easy flow of ideas, and in the works for piano and strings — the Phantasy Quartet, Phantasie Trio and Piano Quintet — the same method of supporting mellifluous string polyphony with simple keyboard figures, often arpeggiated.

None of the works from the period 1906-1912 shows an unusual advance in emotional scope or individuality over its predecessors, although one can point to signs of an increasing structural richness and technical mastery. To talk in general terms about both the technique and emotional scope in the five major chamber works of the period is not to misrepresent them, since they all explore the same restricted territory. On the other hand, the fluency of thought and the ingenuity of structure and thematic working are remarkable, and show Bridge to have been a master of purely musical discourse at a time when the preoccupations of almost all his British contemporaries were mystical and poetically atmospheric. Abstract chamber music occupies a dominating position in his output, although he also contributed examples of nature music and tone poetry which were the equal of anything of the kind written at that time.

One of the most important influences upon Bridge's evolution of personal structural principles was the series of chamber-music competitions organised by W W Cobbett. Cobbett had the stimulating idea of forging a link with the great Elizabethan and Jacobean age of English chamber music by setting up competitions for single-movement, so-called 'phantasies'. He thus did something to combat the automatically accepted four-movement archetype, encouraging a fresh approach to the principle of unity in diversity with a movement that would embrace the different moods and textures of classical precedent by thematic inter-connexion.

In Bridge's case this stimulated an all-important approach to form which remained with him throughout his career. Three of his early chamber pieces were entered for Cobbett's competitions: the Phantasie String Quartet (1901), the Phantasie Piano Trio (1907) — which took a first prize —, and the Phantasy Piano Quartet (1910). The arch-shaped structures he invented in these works cast long shadows: even in pieces which are not in one movement, the phantasy idea can be seen at work, producing in, for instance, the later Cello Sonata, a second movement which combines *adagio* and *finale*.

One of the most radical developments of the principle occurs in the *Rhapsody* Trio for two violins and viola of 1928 (although Rhapsody is a misleading term for this bitingly concentrated single movement). In still subtler relationship to the phantasy arch-form is Bridge's tendency to return to the opening of a work during the closing pages, even when a three-movement layout has been employed, as in the Piano Quintet or the Fourth String Quartet.

The three Phantasy works themselves, however, are uncomplicated examples of formal integration, for all their effectiveness. The Phantasy Piano Trio, with the scheme A (*allegro moderato*) — B (*andante*) — C (*scherzo*) — B — A, and the Phantasy Piano Quartet, A (*andante*) — B (*allegro*) — C (*trio*) — B — A, show the variety of emphases Bridge drew from the form, and also the characteristic vocabulary and syntax of his early period. Both works open with a dramatic challenge and then proceed to a leisurely unfolding of the principal melodic material. In the Trio the subject is stated over an ostinato on the piano which persists for 46 bars (*Ex 1b*). This is typical of the simplicity of Bridge's keyboard writing; and typical, too, is the way the melody moves forward in easy-going periods with a leisurely counter-statement leading to the dominant, and subsequent polyphonic growth.

On paper the repetitive rhythms and the simple modulations may seem naive; but even with such basic material, Bridge already possessed a sense of the broad paragraph which carries the listener easily forward. The *Andante* proceeds by analogy to an easy counter-statement and subsequent imitative sequences, and the climax, typifying Bridge's judgment in the placing of events, comes only after the intervening *Scherzo*.

An important aspect of the Trio's motivic work and transformation is first defined by the dramatic prelude (*Ex 1a*). The following example shows how x generates the opening melodic span (*Ex 1b*), then invades what by now seems to be an independent line (*Ex 1b*), and how later the two components x and y interact to produce a further release of lyrical energy (*Ex 1c*).

The Phantasy Piano Quartet, which comes at the end of what might be called Bridge's first period, shows how he had developed mastery and

Ex. 1b

bis
Vln.
p
x
p
10 bars counterstatement leading to:-
etc.
x
etc.
x

Ex. 1c

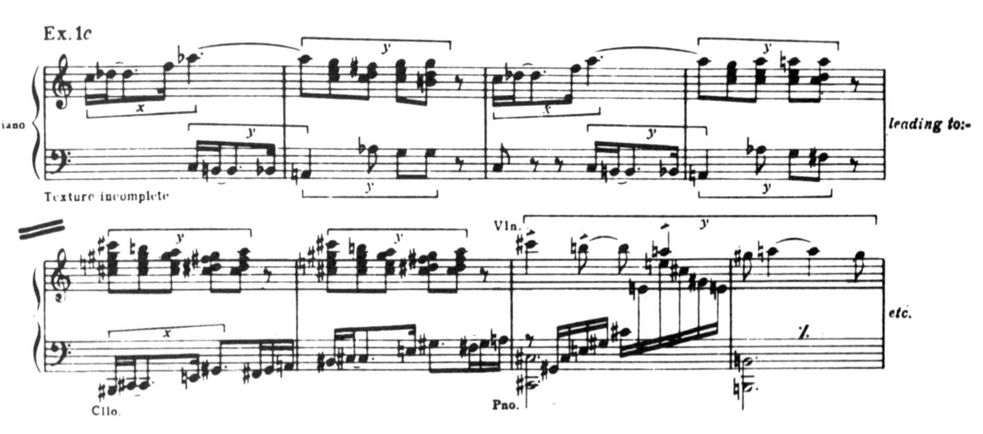
x
y
Piano
y
y
leading to:-
Texture incomplete
y
y
Vln.
y
x
etc.
Cllo.
Pno.

Ex. 2a

assurance without really enlarging his expressive range. The initial melodic span still uses the textbook harmonic vocabulary that perhaps seems a little faded today, while the melody avoids disjunct shapes and chromatic inflections (*Ex 2a*). The supple phrasing, however, is Bridge at his most inventive; and when the counter-statement leads, as in the *Trio*, to expansive polyphonic extensions, we reach one of those heart-warming sequences which are the hallmark of the composer's early manner. The easy contrapuntal mastery with which motive x in *Ex 2b* flows in imitation through beautifully judged modulations can indeed be related to Brahms, different though the sound-world is. The arrival of F major at the end of the example creates a fine sense of elevation, and initiates further lovely melodic growths. Very characteristic of Bridge's harmony at this time are the chromatic sixths in *Ex 2b* — the nearest he gets in his early music to using harmony for sensuous effect rather than as part of the linear argument.

Although the Phantasy Piano Quartet shows early Bridge at his finest, two other works approach it in craftsmanship and breadth: the First String Quartet and the Piano Quintet. The Quartet, named the *Bologna* following its success there in a competition in 1906, is the composer's first large-scale work of real identity, and it brings to a peak his early preoccupation with the string quartet medium, capitalising on the experience gained from writing the Phantasy String Quartet (1901), and the two sets of salon pieces, *Idylls* (1906) and *Novelletten* (1906). It is a work that tells us much about the newly emergent composer, an exceptionally adroit craftsman for a 25-year-old at this period in English music, yet also cautious in what he expects of his players and listeners. There is a revealing lack of those knotty incidents in melody and texture which would suggest the young composer coming to grips with an individual vision. We can perhaps conclude that Bridge was the type of artist whose creative personality was initially founded on a natural gift for composition and a strong feeling for good taste, rather than on a burning sense of his own uniqueness as a human being. That was only to develop later.

Bridge's skill was in advance of all his contemporaries at this time, but his first consideration was accessibility and practicality — admirable tenets if harnessed to pressure of vision, but dangerous when given over-riding importance, compelling the composer to use familiar tags, explore well-charted emotional territories, and smooth all corners and edges. In this way growth can be hindered, and it is not surprising that some saw the composer as 'too professional' in his methods. Luckily for his art Bridge later developed a strong curiosity about styles and techniques outside his immediate world, and allowed his growing store of emotional experience to connect with his compositional mastery. But this is not prefigured in his early music.

Despite these considerations, however, the First Quartet, judged on its own merits, is still an admirable achievement. Although the slow movement, a 'song without words', and the gracious *scherzo* and *trio* are redolent of Bridge's salon style, the opening sonata structure announces the composer's wider aims. It was a mistake to treat the easy-going second subject at length in the development prior to extending it even further during the recapitulation, but the spaciousness of the movement shows Bridge's early sense of musical architecture. This, rather than the invention of immediately memorable individual incidents, was always to be the main embodiment of his thought. Both the intervallic content of the opening theme, for example, and its rhythmic outline prove to be motivically fruitful, and already we find first-movement material clinching paragraphs in the third and fourth movements, a characteristic unifying process.

The Piano Quintet was begun in 1904, before any of the works so far discussed, but in 1912 was drastically revised and shortened. Drawing upon his phantasy experience, Bridge now combined the originally separate *scherzo* and slow movement. Its material is markedly similar in character to that of the two Phantasies, and confirms that this period was a time for perfecting the detail of a largely unchanging vision.

The String Sextet dates from the same period, for Bridge began the work in 1906 but did not complete it until 1912. Texturally it is his most substantial chamber work, and also one of his blandest. But its euphony and absence of conflict are characteristic of even the strongest works of this period. There is seldom a marked contrast between main and secondary ideas, for example: the introduction of new material usually reinforces a mood and flow already established, and the arrival of the recapitulation rarely makes a point of dramatic reinstatement. As in the revised Piano Quintet, one senses that the 'phantasy' was at the back of Bridge's mind while working on the Sextet, since the slow movement incorporates a quasi-scherzo, and the final coda typically combines first- and last-movement material.

The only orchestral work from this period that is generally known is the symphonic suite *The Sea* of 1910-1911, and it does not essentially alter the picture so far established. The range of available instrumental colour probably encouraged Bridge to emphasise sensuous texture and use it as an embodiment of tone poetry — and the work does often suggest visual and poetic imagery. But if the abstract quality characteristic of the chamber music's discourse recedes into the background here, thematicism, clarity of line, and purely musical proportions are still of prime importance. Nevertheless, the symphonic label is not entirely appropriate, for a sense of increasing engagement between the various elements of composition is somehow lacking. The ideas follow each other in picturesque succession, and even when, as in the scherzo, *Seafoam,* two primary themes are harnessed

Ex. 3a

Ex. 3b

Ex. 3c

Ex. 4

Allegretto moderato

in counterpoint, the regular progress is not disrupted. The absence of tension by interaction becomes critical in the final *Storm*, where the tempestuous gestures are painted but the elemental process is not re-enacted in the music.

Bridge seems to have realised at about this time that his musical thinking was one-dimensional in its processes, and that vital areas of his creative imagination had still to be explored. The subsequent journey towards self-discovery, hastened by the evidently traumatic experience of the First World War, was to lead to a final period of radical activity that set in with startling suddenness at the beginning of the 1920s. But, for the time being, his extension of range depended on no more than a growing intensity in all the aspects of his compositional craft, most significantly in his increasingly elaborate chromaticism.

This development can be studied by comparing two orchestral works whose titles suggest a similarity of aim both artistic and technical, but whose substance marks a growing intellectual scope and emotional awareness: the *Dance Rhapsody* of 1908 and the *Dance Poem* composed five years later. The former is an attractive work, full of vigorous invention and by no means inferior to *The Sea* in the quality of its ideas. But for all its vitality, the achievement, like that of *The Sea*, is diminished by a rather easy-going approach to the problem of large-scale form. The work consists of a sequence of four contrasted dance sections, only loosely connected by comparatively routine transitions, and it closes with a return of the opening after a brief dominant preparation. The opening is a pounding six-eight, vigorously symphonic in impetus (*Ex 3a, b,* and *c*), but the second section, rather in the manner of an Austrian *schnadahupfler* (*Ex 4*) (was Elgar's first

17

Ex. 5

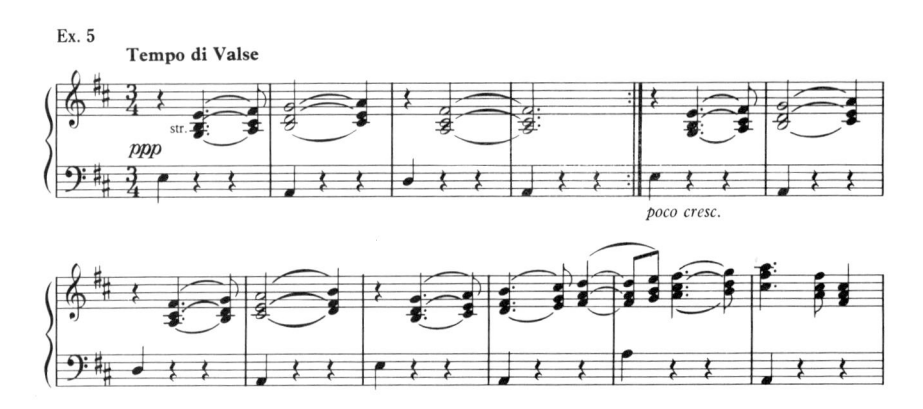

Ex. 6

Ex. 7

Bavarian Dance at the back of Bridge's mind?), and the subsequent *Waltz* (*Ex 5*) and *Polka* (*Ex 6*) sections are more suite-like in treatment. Bridge, out of an innate musicality, ensures a certain overall homogeneity by employing ideas with a family resemblance, even if this only amounts to the similar contours of *Exx 4* and *5*, and the shared head motive of *Exx 4* and *6*. But there is practically no large-scale working of ideas such as we find in the motivically saturated music of his maturity. The only episode that tightens the structural arch and prevents the main body of the work from being a casual diversion is a cogent development of the opening theme which appears in the middle of the *Waltz* (*Ex 7*).

The tuneful, if also naive, quality of invention which characterises the *Dance Rhapsody* has virtually disappeared from Bridge's vocabulary by the time of the *Dance Poem*, and this marks a crucial step forward in his development. In the later work immediately arresting themes are replaced by material whose flexible shapes are designed with a view to motivic transformation and contrapuntal working (*Exx 8a, b, c and d*), and the textures are considerably more chromatic (*Ex 8d*). The contrasted modes of thought are epitomised by the boldly rhetorical opening of the *Rhapsody* (*Ex 3a*) and the eliptical assemblage of motives that launches the *Poem* (*Ex 8a*). The form of the *Poem* is that of symphonic waltz, with a spacious

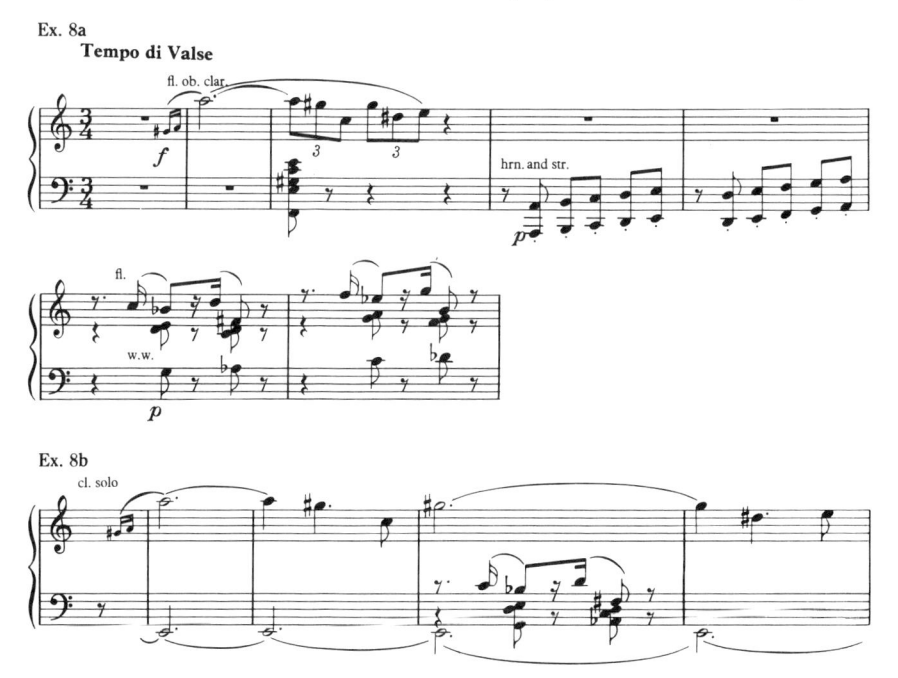

Ex. 8a

Ex. 8b

Ex. 8c

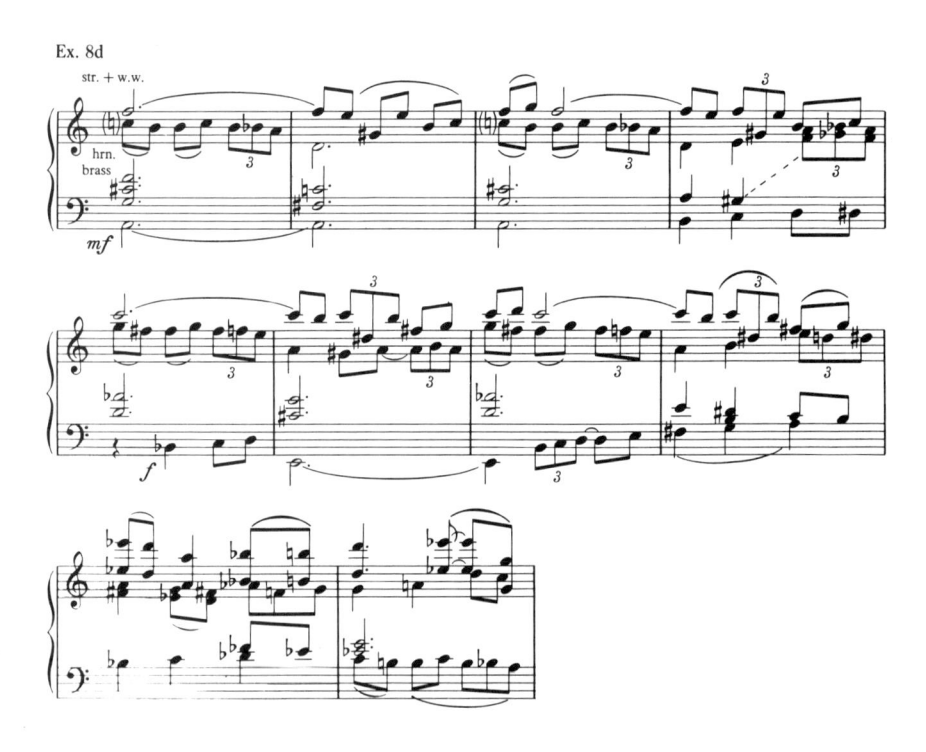

Ex. 8d

introduction and central episode, and its evolutionary processes make it a more concentrated work than the *Rhapsody*. The trouble is that, in attempting greater unity through flexible and determined thematicism, Bridge has failed to provide a sufficiently varied range of ideas. There should have been a greater array of motives or bolder transformations. The main theme and central episode fit together in easy counterpoint for their combined recapitulation, for instance (*Ex 8c*), but the achievement in harnessing such uneventful shapes is perhaps not all that great. *Dance Poem* is nevertheless a significant and encouraging work, offering a glimpse of much broader horizons than we find in his previous music.

The middle period

Four works may be taken as representative of the period when Bridge began building on the transitional achievement of *Dance Poem*: the tone poem *Summer* (1914-1915), *Two Poems* and the Second String Quartet (1915), and the Cello Sonata (1913-17).

Summer already seems to inhabit a more intensely imagined world. The way in which gently insistent figures establish at the outset an aura of concentrated poetry is quite new for Bridge, revealing a ripening sensibility. The melodic flow is still leisurely, and the lyrical main subject undergoes the by now familiar counter-statement and polyphonic growth. But, despite the lazy warmth of the work's poetry, there is a new tension beneath the surface, and much of this has to do with the harmonic textures. Bridge has veered away from the serpentine progressions of the *Dance Poem*, which though interesting in their chromatic syntax were also a little anonymous in tone, and has moved towards the pastoral idiom that in varying degrees served so many of his English contemporaries — an idiom in which diatonic dissonance and modality offset chromaticism. Paradoxically in so doing he managed to tap a deeper and more individual well of feeling, for contact with more harmonically minded composers like Delius, Ireland and Bax greatly enriched a language that had so far concentrated upon developing line and discourse.

Along with this increased harmonic awareness there appear, if only tentatively, juxtapositions of sonority which further the structural arguments, in contrast to the still important melodic and contrapuntal extensions. The orchestral colour-range presumably promoted this tendency, or, again, contact with the formal methods of harmonically-dominated composers — c.f., the mosaic of subtly contrasted sonorities in Delius's *In a Summer Garden*. Compared with the highly unconventional texture-building of Delius, however, Bridge can seem disconcertingly orthodox to the score-reader. The most resplendent climax in *Summer*, a

Ex. 9

paragraph of sustained elevation, reveals part-writing of text-book correctness (*Ex 9*). Nothing could be more characteristic of Bridge than this perfect marriage between technical orthodoxy and genuinely original poetic inspiration.

Without disrupting the pastoral serenity that seems to have occupied Bridge's thoughts at this time, the *Two Poems* for orchestra, which take as their starting points quotations from Richard Jefferies, embody a more complex world of feeling. The first uses as its motto 'Those thoughts and feelings which are not sharply defined, but have a haze of distance and beauty about them, are always the dearest'. It is an enchanting essay in evocation and very revealing of Bridge's increasing scope. The emotional ambivalence behind the hypnotically repetitive harmonic cells (*Ex 10*) is, for instance, typical of the composer's mature thought. Does the heart rejoice in rapt contemplation or regret the ultimate transience of things? The gently poised emotion finds an exact analogy in the harmonic ambiguity whereby a delicately sketched base-line, on harp alone, contradicts the implications of the sustained upper texture. In the middle section we return to a more conventional pastoral manner, the property initially, perhaps, of Butterworth, but the idiom is beautifully handled and assimilated, taking on in context a fresh significance. The second Poem is a little *scherzo* and is headed: 'How beautiful a delight to make the world joyous! The song should never be silent, the dance never still, the laugh should sound like water which runs for ever'. The joyful confidence of the writing gives a

Ex. 10

restrained foretaste of the erruption of similar feelings in *Enter Spring*, and characteristic finger-prints are everywhere to be found, most obviously in the contrapuntal combination of all three main ideas in the final climax (*Ex 11, x, y and z*).

Ex. 11

The seemingly purposeful growth of style which is embodied in *Summer* and the *Two Poems* is not pursued in quite such an orderly fashion by other works from this period. Bridge was capable of looking back as well as forward, and in what was to be the most eclectic stage of his career he also explored modes of thought and execution which were eventually found unsuitable and dropped from his vocabulary.

Bridge's first mature chamber music masterpiece, for example, the Second String Quartet, is more firmly tied to the past than *Summer*, possibly because ideas for the work had germinated over a longer period, or else because the medium encouraged him to rely on the well-tried methods of contrapuntal discourse which were linked to his previous style. The chromatic language certainly marks an advance over the work's chamber music predecessor, the Phantasy Piano Quartet, but there is still something of the blandness of his previous manner. For all its harmonic richness, the first subject of the first movement is typical in this respect, since the chromaticism decorates a firm G minor outline — the theme itself innocent of all accidentals — and the vertical formations avoid those acute tensions which were to characterise his mature writing (*Ex 12*). The second subject, with its spacious succession of accompanying triads, confirms the trend. Nevertheless the quartet is a splendid achievement, whose superb writing for the medium reflects Bridge's practical experience as a professional viola player. There are moments of magical sonority, like the hushed emergence of the finale's main theme from the wistful 'molto adagio' preface; and among the many structural subtleties is the oblique return to the opening subject in the first movement, which is then considerably varied. In the

Ex. 12

finale there is the typical appearance of first-movement material: the first subject is rhythmically transformed in the development, the second supplies the prelude, and the work as a whole teems with the motive derivations which make Bridge's large-scale thought so compelling.

The period covered by the fourth work under consideration, the Cello Sonata, encompasses that of all the middle-period works so far discussed, and each of the trends discovered there features in it. At every stage in his career Bridge's idiom was particularly well integrated — a mark of his technical fastidiousness and unerring taste — but the Cello Sonata confirms that he was opening himself up to an increasingly wide range of stylistic references at this time. The least nationalistic of composers is found at one point employing the folk-song and organum manner, and, less predictably, responding to the flexible melodic shapes of Rachmaninov. If this latter characteristic is thought to be a mere coincidence in two late-Romantic composers (for Bridge was still this), then the second subject of the Second Quartet's first movement also resembles the other composer in its top line and triplet formations. In the broadest sense, however, the Cello Sonata is pure Bridge throughout. The rolling periods of the opening sonata structure constitute the last of those lyrical flights which were initiated by the Piano Quintet and Phantasy Trio; but now the accompaniment fluctuates between support and motivic intrusion which adds richness and tension to the music's progress. The big second movement, which opens with something like a Baxian threnody, develops its chromatic strains with a method and discipline quite unlike that of Bax; and the arch-shaped structure, which incoporates a thematically derived *scherzetto* at the centre, and a strong reference to the work's opening as finale-coda, shows Bridge's formal mastery at its height.

Bridge had now reached a stage in his career where he can be said to have brought his orderly sense of flowing development to a peak. Without breaking with his first-period manner, his textural procedures and melodic writing were acquiring an increased flexibility. He also appeared at this time to be approaching a closer relationship with such composers as Holst and Vaughan Williams. In his only work for chorus and orchestra, *A Prayer* (1916), he released long sequences of first and second inversion triads — a new element in his vocabulary used as extensively as this — while the presence of the chordal motive x in *Ex 13* (cf. Phantasy Quartet, y in *Ex 2b*) reminds us of Holst's *Choral Fantasia* — although typically it provided moments of intensity in a flowing paragraph, while in Holst it is a self-sufficient mystical symbol (Ab C E G).

Even more Holstian is the climax at the words 'love to be despised, and not to be known in this world', where the tritonal pull between the pedal G and the upper harmony suggests the other composer's cataclysmic vision

Ex. 13

Ex. 14

(*Ex 14*). The work is in neatly engineered verse form and is clearly tailored for the amateur choir with part-writing that alternates between the simplest note-against-note texture and conventional imitative counterpoint. Only in a handful of bars does Bridge abandon four parts for multiple divisions. It could be said, in fact, that the choral writing in both line and harmonic texture is lacking in enterprise. But against this must be weighed its unfailing practicability and effectiveness, and, more importantly, the wider-ranging harmony and colour of the orchestral contribution.

Considering the amount of music that Bridge wrote during the first two decades of the century for amateur performers, whether chamber musicians or vocalists, it is perhaps surprising that he made no further efforts to nourish the most important amateur repertory of all. Certainly a body of choral music in his more approachable style might have helped to sustain his reputation in later years, when his increasingly difficult idiom was not only making the composition of music for amateurs virtually impossible, but was also losing him professional patronage.

As yet, however, there were few, if any, indications of the stylistic revolution which lay just ahead, and an informed observer might well have concluded that Bridge was destined to reconcile his cosmopolitan-inclined fluency of thought with the harmonic and textural vocabulary which later generations were to see as typically British. Ultimately, Bridge did indeed effect something of a rapprochement between an English mode of feeling and a broadly-based European language. And yet — for such is the unaccountability of genius — the radical manner in which he achieved it could not have been forseen.

Years of transition

The development of Bridge's language after the Cello Sonata is so arresting that it suggests some kind of inner upheaval. It was associated, perhaps, with his revulsion against war — Benjamin Britten has spoken of his teacher's passionately held pacifist convictions — and very probably there was also the feeling that his own cultural tradition had disappeared in the holocaust, along with so many lives and hopes, compelling him to forge and feel anew, for the alternative of dreaming over a lost past would have been unthinkable to an artist of Bridge's temperament. On the other hand, his developing language at the time of the Cello Sonata and the Second String Quartet may have unlocked some door to his subconscious. Whatever the case, he appears to have experienced a crisis of style, and perhaps even of personality, immediately after the war. It is significant, for instance, that with one exception no major work seems to have been conceived after the completion of the Cello Sonata until the crucially important Piano Sonata, begun in 1922 but not finished until 1925.

That exception is the little opera in three scenes, *The Christmas Rose*, which was sketched in 1919 and scored ten years later. Moments of dramatic pressure elicited a rich harmonic response from Bridge, with splashes of whole- and bi-tonal colouring; but over the work as a whole there lies an idyllic serenity in which the composer seems for the moment to be by-passing the problems which were soon to force themselves upon him. Alternatively, one can perhaps see in Bridge's frequently radiant treatment of a story concerning the journey of the good shepherds and their children to visit the infant Jesus an expression of thanksgiving for the ending of the 1914-18 madness. If that is so, then the subsequent disillusion becomes the more poignant. For the rest, the period between the Cello and the Piano Sonatas was devoted to collections of small piano pieces and a handful of songs, some of which indicate the beginnings of Bridge's new style.

At this point it is perhaps worth touching on Bridge's achievements in this field, for to many musicians they are still the only familiar part of his output. The majority of his piano pieces date from the middle period of his career, for the genre, like that of song, became incompatible with his fully developed late style, and they tend to reflect preoccupations which are more fully explored in the large-scale works of the period. *Solitude*, for instance, composed in 1913 and published as one of *Three Poems*, obviously relates to the chromaticism of *Dance Poem* in its strangely wandering harmony and line, while *Sunset* (1914), from the same group, pressages the mood of the first of the *Two Poems* for orchestra. Prior to the comparative spate of pieces during this period, which probably stemmed from publishers' growing interest in his music, there were few songs and less piano pieces, suggesting that Bridge was always more concerned with the broader structural arguments than with self-contained statement. The delicious *Three Sketches* for piano of 1906, however, prove his ability in the enclosed world of the character piece: *April* is full of a piquant charm which is untainted by the faded air of much Edwardian salon music, as is *Valse Capricieuse* (which perhaps dates from nearer the publication year, 1915), and *Rosemary* begins with something of the delicacy of a Fauré song, developing a tiny *allegro* in its central episode with unobtrusive yet perfectly judged contrapuntal working. Of the *Three Pieces*, composed mostly in 1912, only *Columbine* recaptures the early charm.

The most prolific years for piano music were 1917-18, which saw the composition of the first set of *Miniature Pastorals*, the suite *A Fairy Tale*, the *Four Characteristic Pieces* and the *Three Improvisations* for left hand. The *Pastorals*, beautifully finished, distinctive little pieces for the technically limited, and the suite hold no surprises, but the *Characteristic Pieces* are most arresting, especially in the chromatic piquancy of *Bittersweet* and the impressionism of *Fireflies*, which creates a bitonal whirring out of its appogiatura chords. The *Improvisations* mark a step backwards in idiom, in spite of the vitality of invention in, for instance, *A Revel*, whose irregular phrase-patterns continually surprise; and with the exception of the second group of *Miniature Pastorals* (1921), which continues with considerable success the poetic and technical scope of the first set, Bridge's next groups of pieces, *The Hour Glass* and *Three Lyrics*, pursue unpredictable courses. Thus, of the *Three Lyrics*, *Heart's Ease* (1921) encompasses Bridge's early salon manner, and *The Hedgerow* (1924) something of John Ireland's wistful poetry, while in the humour of *Dainty Rogue* (1922) there is a more typical chromaticism. Clearly the demands of the commercial market were vieing with those inner expressive needs which found a more satisfactory outlet in the Piano Sonata gestating at the same time. It is perhaps for this reason that the slightly earlier sequence of three pieces, *The Hour Glass* (1920), is better integrated stylistically and possesses a more precisely defined poetic character, whether in the pristine freshness of *The Dew Fairy*, or the solemnity of *The Midnight Tide*, with its distant echoes of Debussy's *La Cathédrale Engloutie*.

For all their withdrawn and sometimes melancholy moods, however, these pieces are still recognisably middle-period in style. By the time he was composing the two pieces *Retrospect* and *Through The Eaves*, which comprise *In Autumn* (1924), Bridge's style revolution had really left its mark. In the total, unresolved chromaticism and rich unfamiliar chord formations of the second piece, virtually all in the piano's treble register, we hear an eerie evocation of rustling breezes, dead leaves and creaking rafters, and if *Retrospect* still reminds us a little of John Ireland's brooding, the chromaticism is more determined.

Bridge wrote only six more piano pieces, of which *Winter Pastoral* and *Graziella* make elegant concessions to conservative taste without quite denying the new discoveries. In *A Dedication*, however, the sonorous bitonal harmony of the Piano Sonata's slow movement is called upon to great effect, and much about these late pieces must have puzzled those amateurs they were intended for.

In some ways it is interesting that Bridge should have abandoned salon music at this time. During the first two decades of his career he seems to have been the sort of artist who quite naturally makes concessions to public taste, and was reputedly not the composer, as Cobbett had it, 'to seek to startle or to gain credit (or the reverse) for revolutionary innovations'. Then it was compatible with his easy-going conservatism, but now, from his increasingly radical viewpoint, he must have believed that the simplification required for the amateur market would compromise his artistic integrity.

Much of what has been said of the piano music applies equally to the songs, the composing of which dried up even earlier. The keyboard writing and vocal lines possess all the grace and practicability one expects of Bridge's elegant craftsmanship, but only a handful of items show in choice of text and musical penetration the attributes of the committed song composer. All the songs composed before the crucial post-war years belong predictably to the drawing room. But within this potentially stultifying convention, there are achievements like the wryly humourous use of harmonic variation in *So Perverse* (1905) or the ardent impetus of *Love Went A'riding* (1914), which is heightened by impetuous shifts of key, while that quintessentially Edwardian ballad *Go Not, Happy Day* (1903) derives an innocent charm from the crosscurrents of its accompanying sextuplets. There is also a warming flow of lyricism in *Where She Lies Asleep* (1914), which captures something of the lazy tenderness of the contemporary

Summer, and in *Thy Hand in Mine* (1917) the rapt sequence of diatonic dissonances transforms a rather trite poem. *Strew No More Roses*, on the other hand, characteristically chromatic for its year of composition (1913, the year also of *Dance Poem* and *Solitude*), lacks harmonic vitality.

The post-war years saw the production of several songs of real distinction, possessing the intensity of, say, the best songs of Warlock or Ireland, although none is quite late enough to benefit from Bridge's most concentratedly radical manner. The diatonic dissonance that marked his style for a short period finds a further outlet in the stately Whitman setting *The Last Invocation* (1918), and the next year saw the composition of two of his best songs, the fateful *'Tis But a Week*, whose trampling progress sets 'half a hundred fighting men' in the context of 'the green leaves of May', and *What Shall I Your True Love Tell?*, which sounds a new note of passionate protest in response to Francis Thompson's poem. In contrast, *Into Her Keeping* and the Yeats song, *When You Are Old*, face the ravages of time and loss with a moving serenity.

Bridge's last group of songs belongs to the years of the Piano Sonata, and they share with that work, and the piano pieces contemporary with it, an extreme chromaticism and a restless melancholy spirit. The three Tagore songs, *Dweller In My Deathless Dreams*, *Day After Day* and *Speak to Me, My Love*, epitomise this transitional period. The rich bi-tonal and chromatic harmonies, often explicable as higher dominant discords, still sometimes distantly recall Ireland, but their greater complexity indicates that Bridge was at the very point of making the final stylistic break which actually occurred in the Third String Quartet. The quality of these late songs makes it regrettable that Bridge did not turn his mind to writing an extended cycle in his mature style. The task would have concentrated his growing command of lyrical immediacy and his long-standing mastery of broad musical structure, as *An Die Ferne Geliebte* did Beethoven's.

The full force of Bridge's creative personality at this crucial time erupted in the Piano Sonata, the work which closed his period of transition and made possible the final late flowering. Its radical procedures began a gradual process of alienation from the public and the performers he had served in pre-war years, but we can now see that it also transformed him from a master craftsman (worthy of admiration, but the author of only one or two works of lasting quality) into a creator of commanding originality and power, the composer of a group of chamber works unsurpassed in 20th-century English music, and of five orchestral works the equal of any of their period by native composers.

What made the Piano Sonata such an extraordinary achievement was the energy and determination with which Bridge withstood the pull of conventional tonal language, and developed logically a bitonal harmonic texture throughout large-scale structures. Several of Bridge's English

Ex. 15a
Andante ben moderato

Ex. 15b

contemporaries were sooner or later to enjoy the frisson obtained from bitonal aggregations, but generally these procedures only resulted in a temporary blurring of some unambiguous tonal outline and were simply a form of chromatic decoration. Thanks to his highly systematic approach to composition, Bridge realised the full implications of such harmony and developed it accordingly. *Ex 15a*, for instance, shows an important motive from the Piano Sonata's introduction. The chord sequence here might be explained as a piquant chain of dominant discords. But to Bridge the interval content of the chords suggested opposed tonalities: triads underpinned by alien seconds *Ex 15b*, from the slow movement, show how such chordal entities reverberated in his mind, and produced more explicit bitonal procedures.

While notably broadening his harmonic perspectives, Bridge realised the need for a renewal of structural thought to match the loosening of tonal bonds. The first movement of the Piano Sonata is in arch-shaped sonata form — another offshoot of the phantasy principle which had also influenced the Cello Sonata's first movement, but the phrase structure no longer flows with the old smoothness: it is splintered in a way that ideally embodies the fractured tonal vocabulary. Occasionally the chromatic manner of an earlier Bridge emerges, with a poignancy that suggests a past beyond recall. The integration of such music with more advanced elements is superbly managed, and in the finale Bridge embarks on an heroic and gritty march which sometimes recalls Ireland at his grimmest, while making far more astringent use of fourth chords and bitonal combinations. The effect of the Sonata is bitter and plangent, and its dedication to a young composer killed in the war, Ernest Farrer, hints perhaps at the source of Bridge's new-found expressive power.

The final harvest

The Sonata is a considerable work in its own right, and it points the way to Bridge's subsequent music, both in its intensely troubled feeling and in many aspects of its style and technique. But the retention of his old manner at several points prevents the composer from realising his full potential. Although attempting far more in terms of musical grammar and syntax than, say, either Bax or Ireland would ever have wanted to, the Sonata still belongs to their world in essence. In a less daring composer it might have marked the furthest distance its composer was prepared to travel within an accepted tradition, and have furnished him with an adequate vocabulary for the rest of his life. With Bridge it was a stepping stone, and after its completion he embarked on a series of chamber and orchestral masterpieces in which he found complete release. Their harmonic language and structural precepts can be related distantly to Scriabin, and more positively to Berg and Bartok, and they severed Bridge almost entirely from his English contemporaries at a time of firmly entrenched conservatism.

The first work to show Bridge's late manner in full flight, all impurities filtered out, the implications of his recently framed ideas completely realised, is the Third String Quartet, completed in 1926 — music which approaches the world of the Second Viennese School in its radical procedures,

Ex. 16
Allegro moderato

while remaining utterly personal in tone. The first movement's first subject (*Ex 16*) is typical of the kind of energetic lyricism in which the Quartet abounds: the sense of linear growth is as strong as ever, but the subtle web of tensions which binds the dislocated phrases together is far removed from the old flowing *cantabile*, as is the way in which all twelve chromatic notes are kept in play.

In the vertical aspects of his textures, Bridge approaches a Schoenbergian pantonality, but the lack of semitonal dissonance in the chord spacing and the tendency to select whole-tone and dominant formations gives an individual flavour. Harmonies of this kind are found in the middle-period works, but the speed with which they are now juxtaposed, and the freedom of the linear writing, dictate a totally different logic and create a new sound-world. The harmonic texture is further extended by the introduction of less orthodox chord structures. The superimposition of tritones and fourths favoured by the Viennese school becomes a new characteristic, as do tense Bartokian chords formed from interlocking major and minor thirds.

The structure of the Quartet's three movements shows an increasing richness and complexity of thought. Main material often appears after a period of assembly and preparation. For instance, *Ex 16* follows a nine-bar *andante* introduction and a further nine bars of motive-juggling. Formally, the whole work is dominated by modifications of the sonata principle — arch-shaped in the first movement, and with a rondo refrain in the finale. (It is indicative of the fertility of Bridge's invention that the abundance of material in the finale still leaves room for additional development of the main first-movement themes). An examination of the microstructure of the Quartet reveals startling facts for an English work of the 1920s. Like Schoenberg before him, Bridge realised the significance of a pervasive motive working as a support for developing argument in the absence of orthodox tonality, and extended the principle to the point of integrating vertical and horizontal aspects of the music. The Quartet's opening melodic motive (x in *Ex 17a*) for example, in which the tritone and fifth above the initial B flat are sounded, suggests the two harmonic possibilities fourth supporting or (by inversion) supported by a tritone, transpositions of which immediately appear in the inner parts of bars 5 and 6, and are a prime constituent throughout the work. A transposition of x also supplies a skeletonic outline of the crucial motive C-E flat— G-F sharp (w in *Ex 17a*, and *Ex 16* — bar 2) and, through it, of the bitonal combination of triads, minor with major a tone higher (v in *Ex 17a*), which suffuses the harmonic texture of the Quartet. (This chord is, in fact, an obsession with Bridge and figures prominently in nearly all his late works).

Tracing the motive connections between successive phrases and incidents in the work, one is irresistibly reminded of the tightly packed motive development in pre-12-note works by Schoenberg and Berg. We can best

Ex. 17a

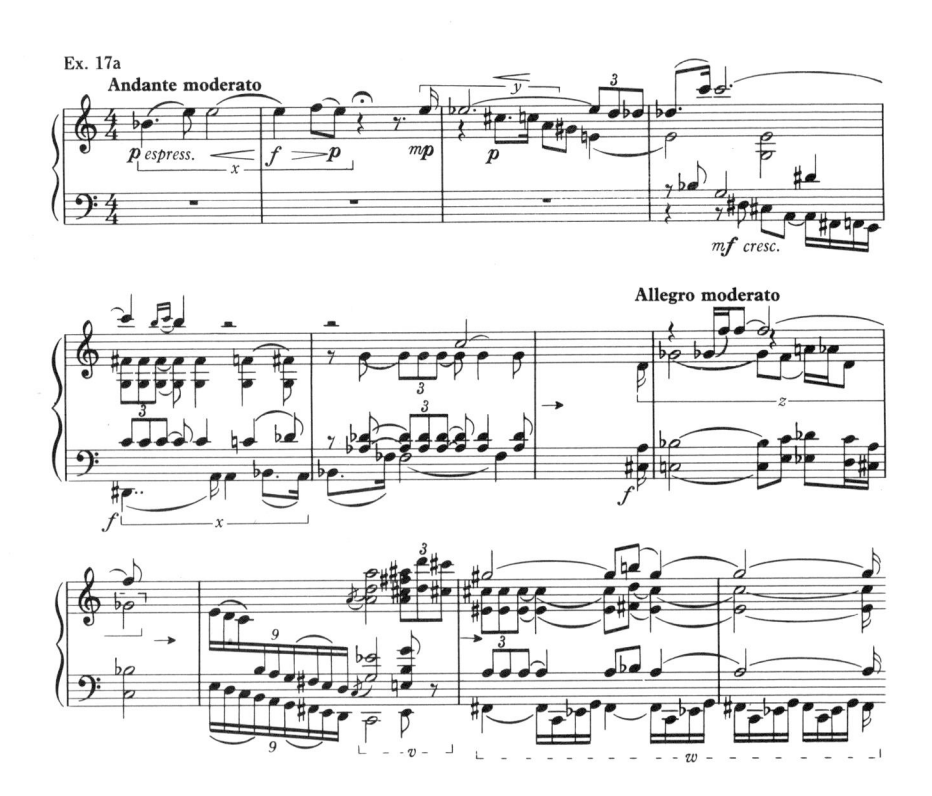

Ex. 17b

see how Bridge's mind worked by comparing the exposition of motives (*Ex 17a*) which precedes the first subject with a tracery of some of the events in the development section (*Ex 17b*). Of special interest is the rearrangement of the scale pattern y in the motive z, indicating a permutational view of material, also the fact that its scale is founded on the fifth and tritone (A-D sharp-E).

The elaborately figured and combative energy of the Third Quartet's outer movements, and the sad, uneasy half-lights of its central intermezzo, inform all the works of Bridge's maturity, and are generally interwoven. But in the two orchestral pieces of the following year these two expressive worlds are separately explored. *There is a Willow Grows Aslant a Brook* is scored for a chamber orchestra of single wind (plus second clarinet), harp and strings and is a miracle of resourceful and atmospheric orchestration.

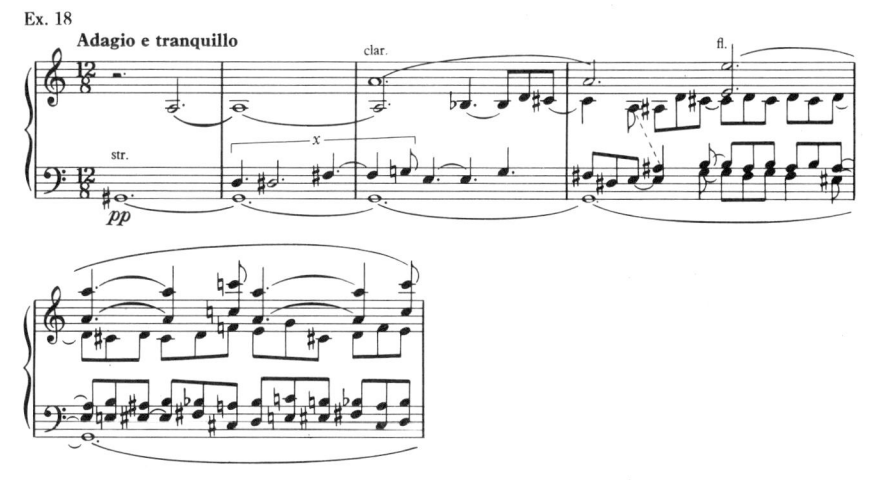

Ex. 18

The form is highly original and its haunted sonority is sustained without monotony, yet with hardly a glimmer of light, by the continual concentrated development of the ideas exposed in the opening bars (*Ex 18*). The little cell x spawns long chains of pitches by means of its interlocking major and minor thirds and semitones. This cell also contains the four most characteristic notes of Bridge's favourite bitonal chord, and this becomes the basis of the threnody for solo strings, itself saturated with the motive thirds, into which the work finally flowers after a bare minimum of literal recapitulation (*Ex 19*).

Ex. 19

Enter Spring, a tone poem for full orchestra, the composing of which Bridge interrupted to write *There is a Willow*, could not provide a greater contrast. It is the composer's most exuberant and untroubled masterpiece, and one of his grandest. After characteristic preliminaries, scintillatingly scored, the main thematic material begins to assemble itself, continually evolving what appear to be definitive statements only to move on to further explorations. *Ex 20* shows one such stream of thought. Three motives, x, y and z, appear in constantly changing relationships while growing new offshoots; and the links in the process are separated by complementary developments.

The energy and breadth of this whole section are prodigious. It leads to a central pastoral of hypnotic beauty in which Bridge's essential Englishness is revealed. This was the last time he was to refer to the unclouded romanticism of earlier years, and that he should have done so after the establishment of his more advanced manner in the Third Quartet is a salutary reminder that no composer's development of style is predictable, even with such an orderly artist as Bridge.

Ex. 20
Allegro moderato

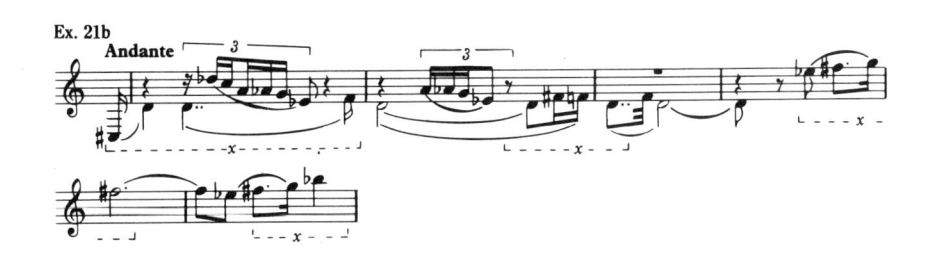

Ex. 21a
Allegro molto

Ex. 21b
Andante

Enter Spring is the only work of Bridge's maturity to avoid the dark, emotionally ambivalent forces which colour the chamber works that followed it, the Rhapsody-Trio (1928), Second Piano Trio (1929), and Violin Sonata (1932).

The *Rhapsody* Trio, for two violins, and viola, shows Bridge's mastery of string sonority at its height, and articulates a private and elusive work which contrasts with the grandeur of statement in the Piano Trio and Violin Sonata. The motive working is no less tight here than in the Third Quartet or *There is a Willow*, the utmost economy of thought giving an impression of rich profusion, and Bridge continues his preoccupation with interlocking major and minor thirds (*x in Ex 21*). A short introduction sets out two basic types of material, quick and slow, both spectral in mood (*Ex 21, a and b*), and there follows a main section of energetically lyrical counterpoint, the two main groups, in what is in effect a seamless flow of music, permeated with motives from the introduction (*Ex 22*). The slow

Ex. 23

Allegro ben moderato

central section, in which the motive thirds eventually assume a more conventionally scalic form, becomes intensely inward, wonderfully personalised by Bridge's command of colour and textural spacing, and after a brief development the main subjects return in their original order — not reversed as in the typical Bridge arch-form (for this is a phantasy in all but name and the composer's most concentrated example). All that remains is for the coda to return the music to the ghostly region of the opening, and there the work evaporates. At no point has the restricted compass of the music limited its emotional scope; indeed it is turned to great expressive account, and the Trio numbers with Bridge's most subtle and individual creations, as many-sided in its way as more ambitious achievements.

In the *Rhapsody* Trio, Bridge uncovers deeper layers of his musical soul. If parts of the Third Quartet reveal, for all his independence of mind, an allegiance with the Second Viennese School, the Trio inhabits an unprecedented world. The individuality of vision which made such a work possible, now expanded magnificently to produce the masterpiece which confirms Bridge as a composer of international stature, the Second Piano Trio. This Olympian work is laid out on the broadest lines, consisting, unusually for Bridge, of a pair of interlinked movements. Once again, the evolution of the melodic lines depends on characteristically related major and minor thirds, and again this idea is expressed vertically in terms of bitonally combined triads, the first two movements concentrating on linear expansion, the third on harmonic and the finale on tieing together previous developments.

Ex. 24

Ex. 25

Ex. 26

At the outset Bridge launches a magnificently sustained flight of lyrical counterpoint, offsetting the tight corners in his searching melodic lines with the piano's open fifths (*Ex 23*). As so often in this work, and throughout late-Bridge, it is easy to demonstrate the compositional mastery behind a process, but not the sheer individuality of the sonority and the thinking, whose rarified passion is difficult to relate to any other composer. A marvellously intensified counterstatement, coming to earth after the stratospheric opening, reminds us with a shock how far Bridge had travelled since the Phantasy Piano Trio's exposition and counterstatement over a keyboard ostinato. The bitonal aspects of the work's ubiquitous thirds come to the fore in the middle section, where a wandering theme (*Ex 24*) banishes all feeling of time with a chain of passacaglia-like repetitions and variations, continuing the discreet *allegretto* of the opening. The recapitulation builds to a majestic climax, where, after an allusion to the middle section, Bridge with consummate timing releases the vast accumulation of tension with a mere eight bars of explosive *allegro*. The movement ascends into a serenity that can only be compared with the Holst of *Betelgeuse*. The linked scherzo wrings fresh shapes from the pattern of thirds (*Ex 25*), and develops the idea of ostinato repetition to a machine-like pitch. We feel that faced with an experience too painful to articulate, emotions freeze over and automatic processes aid the afflicted sensibilities. There is an interlude theme (*Ex 26*) in which the piano's right hand superimposes a more relaxed, quasi-modal line of thirds over the original tighter shape, and the centre of the movement (the trio, perhaps) is taken up with an expansive new melodic paragraph replete with motive thirds (*Ex 27*) — all these ideas punctuated and carried forward by the *scherzando* figures (*Ex 27*).

Ex. 27

We are drawn even deeper into the aftermath of some searing experience in the haunting slow movement. Again there is the endless ticking of an ostinato rhythm, decked out now with rich bitonal harmony (*Ex 28a*). The main section is built from a sequence of little harmonic cells, each constructed from one of two bitonal combinations: minor triad with major a tone higher (the 'Bridge chord'), or major and minor sharing the same mediant. In the short central episode, part really of an unbroken span, the triads become augmented, combined only if they belong to the same whole-tone scale, and the melodic strands proliferate densely (*Ex 28b*). The finale weaves all these threads together in a sonata *allegro*. The opening subject (*Ex 29*) focusses on the 'Bridge chord', which supports a top line of characteristic thirds, and these thirds also permeate the second subject. Then, first-movement material combines with a subsidiary theme of the finale in the development which leads to a direct quotation of the Trio's opening. This momentarily draws the music away from passionate engagement, but a return of the initial impetus brings with it the recapitulation, building a tumultuous climax which floods over into a restatement of the first movement's second theme. There is a sense of heroic attainment here, but the victory is hardly a comfortable one and the music withdraws poignantly to the heights it had occupied at the outset.

Ex. 28a

Ex. 28b

Ex. 29

[musical notation: Allegro, bis]

The Violin Sonata is hardly less impressive. Its single span goes much further than that of the *Rhapsody* Trio by embracing the four movements of traditional usage in sequence — sonata *allegro* exposition; *andante*; *scherzo*; recapitulation-cum-finale — yet integrating this apparently looser structure with the customary motive derivations. The two middle movements, for example, quote the exposition's main themes at key moments, as well as evolving their own ostensibly new material from the same source. The melodic and harmonic processes are less rigorously schematic than in the two trios, but are full of characteristic finger-prints like the familiar linked major and minor thirds — an astonishingly productive idea which always sounds newly minted. In fact, in personality and style the Sonata seems more closely related to the energetic lyricism of the Third Quartet than to the withdrawn or monumental expression of its immediate predecessors.

Bridge's output of chamber music was completed by two characteristic works, the Fourth String Quartet (1937) and *Divertimenti* for wind quartet (1934-38). The String Quartet, which marks perhaps the peak of his writing in the genre, resembles its predecessor in certain respects. There is a similar vein of lyrical energy to that shown in *Ex 16*, and the central movement is again a wistful intermezzo. But it is now in the finale that a slow introduction leads, via an assembly of motives, to a definitive thematic statement, and its rondo structure presses to a conclusion of hard-won optimism, contrasting with the melancholy into which the Third Quartet descends. In more general terms, the language has moved away from the expressionist richness of its predecessor: a more classical vision is outlined by the concentrated statements, concise transitions, and increased economy of texture. At the same time there is room enough for lyrical growth, and the first movement's second subject can afford counterstatements, albeit in

Ex. 30
Allegro energico

varied forms, which remind us of Bridge's early expansive vein. There is also space for the obligatory references to the first-movement material as the work closes. In its harmonic world the Fourth Quartet is the most radical of all Bridge's works, and its preoccupation with the more open intervals — fourths, fifths, major thirds and ninths — gives a new textural personality, uncompromisingly dissonant and bracing (*Ex 30*). The old obsession with interlocking thirds has left its mark, but the composer's

Ex. 31
Allegro con brio

harmonic resources are becoming increasingly wide-ranging, and the masterly way in which he saturates the texture of the finale with fifths, the interval of optimism and tonal orientation, using overtone structures to suggest a high norm of polytonal dissonance, typifies the new freedom (*Ex 31*).

Divertimenti confirms Bridge's classical trend and develops his elusive, at times almost fugitive, manner. Although true to its title in scope of feeling, it is a toughly argued work, laconic in statement, and prone to neo-classical rhythmic contours. There are four movements, of which the middle two are duets, for flute and oboe, and clarinet and bassoon respectively. The first movement, which could be sub-titled 'Fanfare, Pastoral and Miniature March', reconciles perfectly the suite-like succession of ideas characteristic of the divertimento with a rigorous development of motive cells. The opening fanfare exposes a group of eight notes consisting of major thirds and their inversions, linked by false relation (*Ex 32a*), and then briefly

Ex. 32a

Ex. 32b

develops it. A little pastoral ensues, characterised by fourths (giving a slightly Hindemithian flavour) and leading to a return of the opening bars. At this point a simply varied recapitulation might have been expected; but by means of thematic transformation Bridge launches an apparently new section, greatly extending the frontiers of the structure — a brief march which re-orders the content of the eight-note group (*Ex 32b*). References to the pastoral fourths provide a tiny trio. The second movement, *Nocturne*, is in Bridge's haunted mood, a rather loose-limbed improvisatory piece, and the third, *Scherzetto*, is drily repetitive, the only dull music Bridge wrote in his maturity. Invention returns to normal in the final *Bagatelle*, however, producing a movement that hovers between skittish humour and something nearer to apprehensive flight.

The orchestral works from the final decade of Bridge's life are unknown to all but a few musicians and enthusiasts. Two of them — *Oration*, a 'Concerto Elegiaco' for cello and orchestra (1930), and the overture *Rebus*

(1940) — are still in manuscript; while the third — *Phantasm* for piano and orchestra (1931) — is only available as a two-piano score. Each is a work of mastery and unmistakeable presence. *Phantasm* is perhaps the easiest to relate to the music so far discussed for, as its title suggests, it explores the twilight world so dear to Bridge. The elaborate ternary form unfolds after an improvisatory introduction which defines the basic premises and (despite a long solo '*quasi improvisando*') establishes the piano in an atmospheric and decorative role rather than as the traditional protagonist of a concerto. Dream-like images are suggested by prominent melodic tritones and whole-tonal and bitonal textures, and a nightmarish feeling begins to take over as a result of the strange motion of the *allegro*. Continuous semi-quavers on the piano (and occasionally in the orchestra) give the impression of running while remaining rooted to the spot, and lend a weird significance to the main theme (*Ex 33a*) which arrives, dark on the bassoons, after a typical period of motivic assembly. It is related to the pastoral shape of *Enter Spring*'s central melody, but the piano's relentless ostinato throws a haunted light on this image of the past. After a counterstatement, with the piano in parallel open fifths, the tutti further distorts the theme with bitonal polyphony, the persistent semi-quavers now

Ex. 34

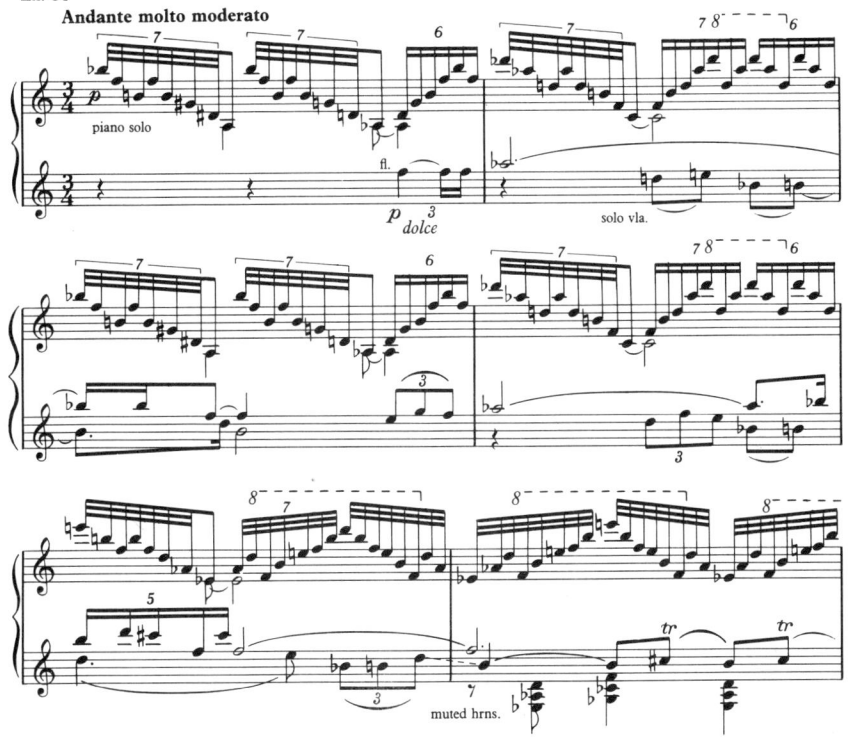

prominently high in the texture (*Ex 33b*), and a *scherzando* second group capriciously transforms the material of the atmospheric introduction, concentrating on its falling tritones G-C sharp, and D sharp-A. The central section moves through an eerie dreamscape, evolving fresh combinations from the same material (*Ex 34*) while also extending it and introducing a new chant-like melody. The recapitulation is comparatively orthodox, but prepares the way for a climactic fulfilment of the principle of nightmarish distortion. *Ex 33a*, becoming increasingly insistent, erupts on full brass over battering timpani, while octave Ds on wind and strings mark the down-beats. The vision is intensified by the addition of a single contrapuntal strand on the tuba, after which the music subsides into the mysterious depths from which it arose.

Phantasm is not an unflawed work. Some of the piano solo interludes are casually transitional, suggesting, a little too readily, hands wandering idly over the keyboard: but in its great breadth of style, defined by simple themes, sometimes weirdly distorted, as well as by totally chromatic textures and lines, it presents a quite extraordinary vision, struck with a haunted beauty, bizarre and sometimes fearful. In this and several other works of the period, Bridge seems to have given birth to and sustained a brand of English expressionism whose only precedents are found in some van Dieren or in Warlock's *The Curlew*.

Oration counterbalances this expression of the darker side of Bridge's nature. Monumental in its power and thematic energy, rather than poetically atmospheric or expressionist, it is nevertheless suffused with the emotional ambivalence of Bridge's mature thought. While appearing to be public in its rhetoric and sense of solemn celebration, it belongs in a deeper sense to a private world, and the opposition of cello — that most speaking and, at times, inward of instruments — and orchestra perfectly embody this concept. The work is, in fact, a funeral address over the lost of the 1914-18 war, and contrasts a deep personal grief with occasional grandeur and images of war. It is by implication a passionate indictment.

Formally, it is quite distinct from *Phantasm*, for it owes nothing to the symphonic poem design but is the last and grandest example of Bridge's phantasy arch-from. The work provides countless examples of the composer's flexible motive development, and much of its material is drawn from the opening of its expansive introduction (*Ex 35a*): the constituent thirds of the triads bound by false relation are of paramount importance, as can be seen from the beginnings of both the first and second subjects of the main section (*Ex 35b and c*). The chief elements of the introduction are a long solo recitative supported by Ex 35a's triads, and a processional, also built from the triads, over a wrong-note ground bass. March-like images figure prominently in the work's ceremonial atmosphere, and the central section, which is loosely developmental, consists of a bizarre march, as of platoons of the dead, underpinned by the timpani's persistent four-in-a-bar on a pedal G. The cello's capricious tune is taken over by two piccolos and oboe, producing a fife-like ostinato against which the first subject is recalled.

The main section and its recapitulation come nearer to traditional concerto concepts than does *Phantasm*: the first subject, energetically stated and extended by the soloist, leads to a powerfully contrapuntal tutti, and the second group shares material between cello and orchestra. The order of subjects, true to the principles of the phantasy sonata arch, is reversed upon recapitulation, and the second theme follows immediately on the heels of the receding march of the middle section. After a short cello cadenza the first group, greatly concentrated, brings a resurgence of energy — indeed, a continuation of development, for the contrapuntal activity is increased, and the second theme is drawn into the polyphonic fabric. At this point the introductory processional returns in full orchestral panoply, and the work's initial triads eventually die away, apparently closing the arch form. However, there follows an unexpectedly long and haunting epilogue: 55 bars of sparsely textured andante threaded on an unbroken C-D harp ostinato. Here the work enters a new expressive area, calm yet withdrawn in its mourning, which greatly expands the imaginative scope of an already spacious masterpiece.

Oration is one of the pinnacles not only of Bridge's art but of 20th-century British music. Indeed it can be placed with the finest orchestral works of the first half of the century, for in its inspired blend of the unpredictable with the logical and orderly, in its perfection of utterance, and in its large-scale control of contrasting tensions, it bears the hall-mark of a classic.

Bridge's last work, the overture *Rebus*, strikes out unpredictably on a new path, not, as one might have expected, drawing on the radical harmonic and thematic style established in the Fourth Quartet, for the forward-looking tendencies of Bridge's mature thought nearly always found their most concentrated and uncompromising expression in the chamber music. On the contrary, what is special to *Rebus* is the way in which characteristically rigorous motive operations are carried out on a much simpler, tonal idea. The work was originally to have been called *Rumour*, until Bridge realised that the war had lent the word sinister overtones, since the principle expressive idea is of a theme which is progressively varied and distorted, as it is passed from instrument to instrument. Appropriately what evolves is a monothematic sonata structure, everything of importance

Ex. 36a

Ex. 36b

Ex. 36c

Ex. 36d

Ex. 36e

Ex. 36f
Allegro vivo

f p 133 str   + ww

stemming from the opening three bars (*Ex 36a*). Some of the most important stages in its transformation are indicated in *Ex 36b*, from later in the introduction, c, the first subject, d, the second, e, the development, and f, the coda.

After more than a decade of inward-looking music that had increasingly estranged him from his public, Bridge was clearly attempting a greater directness and simplicity of utterance in *Rebus*. The unclouded and triumphant C major of the second subject, for example, is unprecedented in his late years (*Ex. 36d*). In reconciling such flowing statements with the elliptical and dislocated phraseology found in, say, the coda, a texturally attenuated section with sudden pauses and abrupt punctuation, Bridge shows his customary mastery. The essentially extravert and ultimately compromising gesture of *Rebus* may have pointed to new departures. But if one is to speculate on what Bridge — ever the explorer — might have achieved had he not died a year later, still in his early sixties and clearly at the height of his powers, one surely sees him building on the radical achievement of the Fourth Quartet, combining breadth of style with concision.

In coming years it may be seen as a tragedy for English music that Bridge was not allotted another 15 years of full creative vigour. Apart from greatly enriching the chamber music and orchestral repertories, he would have lived on into an era where he would have connected with a less hide-bound generation of young composers, the only senior figure who had faced up to the most advanced continental developments and proved that an English composer of integrity could emerge from the experience not only unscathed but immeasurably enriched.

Page from the score of 'Enter Spring' to be published in 1976 by Faber Music Ltd.

*Above: Frank and Ethyl Bridge with the young Benjamin Britten.
Below: The Bridge home at Friston.*

A newspaper drawing, dating from 1927.

CATALOGUE OF WORKS

LEWIS FOREMAN

This catalogue has been prepared by first collating together a number of catalogues, both published and unpublished. The resultant composite list was then edited in the light of the printed music so far as it could be inspected in the Central Music Library (London) and the writer's own personal collection. This master-list was then compared to the huge collection of manuscripts in the Parry Room at the Royal College of Music, London, details of most of which had already been incorporated, by virtue of Oliver Davies' catalogue listed below. A questionnaire was also circulated to all present or past publishers of Bridge's music, and much useful information was added in this way.

Catalogues that have been taken into account in this work are:

British Library: [Unpublished, guard-book catalogue] Music since 1800.
BBC Music Library: Orchestral catalogue (inspected at Central Music Library).
ASCAP: Catalogue of orchestral music.
New York Public Library: Music collection.
Boosey & Hawkes: A typescript catalogue compiled for me by Carol A. Davies, archivist.
A catalogue (believed to have been compiled in collaboration with Bridge himself) published in the *Musical Times* Feb. 1919.
The catalogue in the fifth edition of *Grove*.
Galliard pianoforte stock list (c 196?).
Boosey & Hawkes: orchestral catalogue 1974.
An unpublished catalogue of the manuscript collection in the Parry Room by Oliver Davies and Kenneth Hayle, 1962.
'The Songs of Frank Bridge', by R. Keating (DMA Thesis, at the University of Texas and Austin, 1970).
(University Microfilms, order no. 71-84)

ORCHESTRATION

The orchestration of orchestral works is designated in the following sequence: flute/oboe/clarinet/bassoon — horn/trumpet/trombone/tuba — percussion harp timpani strings.
Thus, 2221 — 4230 — hp timp str, means two each of flutes, oboes and

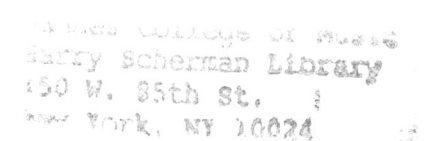

clarinets, one bassoon — four horns, three trumpets, two trombones, no tuba, harp, timpani and strings.

Where instruments are doubled by the same player they are added in parentheses. Thus in the above example, if the first group had been designated 2(1),2(1),2(1),2(1), it would have indicated that of the two flutes the second doubled on piccolo, oboes with cor anglais, clarinets with bass clarinet and bassoons with contra bassoon, and this pairing was reflected in the orchestral parts.

If, however, a plus sign (+) had been used, this would have signified an extra player and an extra part would be provided. Thus, 2(+1), 2(+1), 2(+1), 1(+1)-43(+1)20 means two flutes, one piccolo, two oboes, one cor anglais, two clarinets, one bass clarinet, one bassoon, one contra bassoon, four horns, three trumpets, one cornet, and so on.

Percussion are listed, and the following abbreviations have been used:

bd = bass drum
cas = castanets
cym = cymbals
glock = glockenspiel
hp = harp
orch = orchestra

pf = piano
sd = side drum
str = strings
tr = triangle
timp = timpani

vib = vibraphone
sax = sax
Gong and celesta are spelled out in full.

RCM = Royal College of Music

FIRST PERFORMANCES

In the case of many of the orchestral works, abbreviated details of the first performances were to be found annotated on the autograph manuscript or with press cutting in marked copies of printed scores, and these have been included in the present catalogue, although no detailed search has been made to trace the dates of all first performances.

PUBLISHERS

Almost all Bridge's publishers have changed since his death. Those interested in works located in the Parry Room should contact the Frank Bridge Trust (at the RCM) if a performance is being considered; otherwise the following table should enable the present owners of performing materials to be traced:

Augener *later* Galliard *now* Stainer & Bell
J. Curwen *now* Faber Music
Hawkes & Sons *now* Boosey & Hawkes
Keith Prowse *now* EMI Music
Winthrop Rogers *now* Boosey & Hawkes
Schirmer works of First World War vintage were republished by Winthrop Rogers, *now* Boosey & Hawkes
Joseph Williams *later* Galliard *now* Stainer & Bell

Works published by Stainer & Bell are still available from that firm, while former Augener publications should be available in the United States from Galaxy.

TIMINGS

Timings have been included where known. In some cases a range of timings are given and these indicate the fastest and slowest performances known. Where timings have been given in catalogues consulted in the compilation of the present catalogue they have been noted, but many timings have come from the compiler's timing of the many recent performances of Bridge that there have been.

ACKNOWLEDGEMENTS

In compiling this catalogue I have received much help from those with an interest in Bridge. Firstly, without the co-operation of the staff of the publishers of Bridge's music in returning my questionnaire I would have been seriously hampered. Secondly, the staff at the Parry Room were most helpful and I am grateful to them in facilitating my access to the Bridge works preserved there. Dr Trevor Bray has pointed out two references in the *Musical Times* to works that I have been unable to trace otherwise, and Paul Hindmarsh (who is writing a thesis on Bridge) checked a draft of this catalogue and made many suggestions for additions and improvements. Finally, my colleagues who have written other parts of this publication have been continual sources of advice. To all of these helpers, my thanks.

ORIGINAL WORKS

Adagio *see* [Two] **Movements for String Quartet**
1 **Adagio in E major for organ**
   Novello 1905; reissued as no 2 of [Three] Pieces for Organ *qv*
2 **Adoration** (*Asleep! O sleep a little while*) — song for voice & piano or orch., wds-Keats (Nov 1905). Originally called "Asleep!"
   Published (voice & piano) Winthrop Rogers 1918; Boosey & Hawkes. Orchestral version on hire from Boosey & Hawkes (2332-4231-timp-str)
   MS: two known — Peter Pears, Boosey & Hawkes
   Timing 3'
   Allegretto *see* [Three] Miniature Pastorals set 1 No 3
   Allegretto Grazioso (for organ) *see* [First] Book of Organ Pieces — 1
3 **Allegro Appassionato** (for viola & Piano)
   Stainer & Bell (*Viola Library*, edited Lionel Tertis, no 2) 1908
   Allegro ben Moderato (for organ) *see* [Second Book of] Organ Pieces — 3
   Allegro Commando (for organ) *see* [First] Book of Organ Pieces — 2
4 **Allegro con Spirito in Bb major** (for organ)
   Novello 1905; reissued as no 2 of [Three] Pieces for Organ *qv*
   Allegro Marziale (for organ) *see* [First] Book of Organ Pieces — 3
   All Things That We Clasp *see* [Four] Lyrics
5 **Amaryllis** (for violin & piano)
   Winthrop Rogers 1919; Boosey & Hawkes
   L'Amour Fugitiv *see* [Two] Songs — French version
6 **Andante Con Moto** (for organ)
   Published in *The Organ Loft*, Book 110, no 329 (1901); collected in [Second] Book of Organ Pieces *qv*
7 **Andante Moderato in C minor** (for organ)
   Novello 1905; reissued as no 1 of [Three] Pieces for Organ *qv*
8 **Andantino** (for organ)
   Published in *The Organ Loft*, Book 103, no 308 (1901); collected in [Second] Book of Organ Pieces *qv*
   April *see* [Three] Sketches (for piano) — 1
9 **Arabesque** (for piano)
   Augener 1916; Stainer & Bell
   Asleep (song) *see* Adoration

10 **Autumn** (part-song SATB) words by Shelley
Novello (first published as supplement to *Musical Times* 1903)
Bagatelle *see* Divertimenti — 4
11 **Berceuse** (for orch; violin & orch; piano; violin & piano; cello & piano) (1902).
Keith Prowse (piano) 1929); (violin & piano, *or* cello & piano) 1902.
Set of four parts (vln I & II, vla,cello/bass) 1902.
Piano conductor & parts (1121-200-str) Keith Prowse 1929; also arr H. Bath (PC — 112(3 sax)1-2230-per-str, on hire from Keith Prowse
MS full score & 14 orchestral parts (Parry Room) 2,2+1,22-400-str
Timing 2' 15"
12 **Berceuse** (*The days are cold, the nights are long*) — song for soprano & piano or orch., wds-Wordsworth (17 Oct 1901)
MS voice and piano score, with some indication of orchestration, plus 25 orchestral parts (2,1+1,2,2,4000 timp str) (Parry Room) unpublished
1st performance RCM 20 June 1902
Bittersweet *see* Character Pieces
13 **Blow, Blow Thou Winter Wind** — song for voice & piano, wds-Shakespeare (1903)
Schirmer 1916; Winthrop Rogers; Boosey & Hawkes
14 **Blow Out, You Bugles** — song for tenor & piano or orch., wds-R Brooke (May 1918)
Winthrop Rogers 1919 (voice and piano)
MS voice and piano (Parry Room); 'Fair copy as used by Gervase Elwes (Parry Room); ms copy — not autograph (Boosey & Hawkes); parts not traced
This song can be sung with piano and trumpet (as recorded on SHE 513)
'Bologna' Quartet *see* String Quartet no 1
Canzonetta (for piano or orchestra) *see* [Two] Entr'actes
15 **Capriccios for piano**
No 1 in A min, Augener 1905; Stainer & Bell. No 2 in F sharp min, Augener 1917
Timing no 1:2' 40"
Carmelita *see* Vignettes de Dance
16 **Cello Sonata** (for cello & piano)
Sketches for an early cello sonata are preserved in the Parry Room
17 **Cello Sonata** (for cello & piano) (1913-1917)
Winthrop Rogers 1918; Boosey & Hawkes
Timing 22' 45"

Chant de Gaiete *see* [Three] Morceux d'orchestre
Chand d'Esperance *see* [Three] Morceux d'orchestre
Chant de Tristesse *see* [Three] Morceux d'orchestre

18 **Characteristic Pieces for Piano** (1915); no 1 *Water Nymphs*; no 2 *Fragrance*; no 3 *Bittersweet*; no 4 *Fireflies*
Winthrop Rogers 1917; Boosey & Hawkes
Cherry Ripe *see* [Two] Old English Songs

19 [A] **Christmas Dance:** Sir Roger de Coverley (for strings) (1922)
String quartet parts, Augener 1922; miniature score, Augener 1923; miniature score (strings), Augener 1939
Timing 4' 30"

20 [The] **Christmas Rose** — opera in three scenes (1919-1929); libretto based on a play for children by Margaret Kemp-Welch and Constance Cotterell
Augener (vocal score) 1931; (chorus part) Augener 1931
Negative photostat of autograph full score (Parry Room) sop/mezzo/ten/bar/bass-bar/female ch/SATB chor. 2222-2210-timp tr/cym bells hp str
Timing 45' 00"
Columbine *see* [Three] Piano Pieces

21 **Come to Me in My Dreams** — song for voice & piano, wds-Matthew Arnold (1906)
Winthrop Rogers 1918; Boosey & Hawkes

22 **Concerto Elegiaco** *see* Oration
Con Moto (for violin & piano) (16 April 1903)
Unpublished
MS Parry Room

23 **Coronation March** (Nov 1901)
Unpublished, unperformed; MS full score (Parry Room): 2+1,2220-4231 timp bd sd cym str

24 **Coronation March** (1911)
Unpublished, unperformed; MS full score (Parry Room): 2+1, 2+1, 2+1, 2+1 -4331- timp st tr cym bd str
(In a paper envelope bearing the following in Bridge's hand: 'Coronation March <u>Damn</u>!')

Country Dance *see* Short Pieces for Violin & Piano — 4

25 **Cradle Song** ('What does little birdie say?') — song for voice & piano, wds-Tennyson (?1904)
Unpublished

26 **Cradle Song** (for violin & Piano or cello & piano)
Goodwin & Tabb 1911

Dainty Rogue *see* [Two] Lyrics — 2

27 **Dance Poem** (for orchestra) ('Sketch Jan-March 1913; finished 30 July 1913')
MS full score & parts (Parry Room): 2+1,2+1,2+1,2+1 - 4,2+2, 31-timp cel tr gong tamb sd bd 2hp str; unpublished ('Performed at Wood's Beethoven concert, Friday 1 Sept 1939 [the] Night Hitler invaded Poland' [Bridge conducted his own work])

28 **Dance Rhapsody** (for orchestra) (May 1908)
Unpublished; MS full score & parts (Parry Room): 2+1,222-4231-timp tr sd bd gong cym celesta hp str
Timing 15'
First performance RCM 31 July 1908

Dawn and Evening (song) *see* (Four) Lyrics

Day After Day *see* [Three] Songs (Tagore); [Four] Songs

29 [A] **Dead Violet** (*The odour from the flower is gone*) — song for voice & piano, wds-Shelley (21 March 1904)
Unpublished

30 **Dear, When I Look** — song for voice & piano, wds-Heine (27 June 1908)
Unpublished

31 [A] **Dedication** (for piano)
Augener, 1928

32 [The] **Devon Maid** (*Where be you going, you Devon Maid*) — song for voice & piano (July 1903), wds-Keats
Published in *The Vocalist* 1905; Boosey & Hawkes; Winthrop Rogers

[The] **Dew Fairy** *see* The Hour Glass — 2

33 [A] **Dirge** (*Rough wind that moanest loud*) — song for voice and piano, wds-Shelley (7 April 1903)
Unpublished

34 **Divertimenti** (for flute, oboe, clarinet, bassoon): no 1 *Prelude*; no 2 *Nocturne*; no 3 *Scherzetto*; no 4 *Bagatelle* (1934-1938)
Boosey & Hawkes, miniature score (Hawkes Pocket Score no 9) 1940, 1951; (Parts) Boosey & Hawkes (1940)
MS Boosey & Hawkes (another Holograph is in the Library of Congress)
'Sketch' for two divertimenti for flute and oboe dated July 1934 and 13 June 1934, plus fair copy, are in the Parry Room

35 **Dramatic Overture** (c 1906)
Lithographed copies of the autograph string parts *only* (Parry Room); score & remaining parts lost

Dusk *see* [The] Hour Glass — 1

Dweller in my Deathless Dreams *see* [Three] Songs (Tagore); [Four] Songs

36 **Easter Hymn**, Ein fröhlicher Gesang — sacred song for voice & piano
English wds-H Wagemann
Chappell & Co (in C & Eb) 1912
MS Destroyed in Chappell's 1964 fire
Also arranged for mixed voices, Chappell 1930

37 **[An] Easter Hymn** (arranged for flute, string quartet, bells & organ by John Foulds) c 1918
Unpublished set of parts: estate of John Foulds
Ecstasy *see* [Three] Poems
E'en As A Lovely Flower *see* [Four] Lyrics

38 **Élégie for cello & piano**
Goodwin & Tabb 1911

39 **En Fête, for piano** (Nov 16 1925)
Unpublished; MS Parry Room *see also* 176

40 **Enter Spring:** rhapsody for orchestra (1927)
Unpublished; score & parts (hire Faber — see page 52) 3333-4331-timp bells, glock, tr, gong,sd,cym bd tamb,celesta 2 hp str
MS Faber
Timings 20'/16' 45"

41 **[Two] Entr'actes** (for small orchestra): no 1 *Rosemary* (1121-2200-timp hp str, *also* arr strings, *also* arr timp, vibra hp str); no 2 *Canzonetta* (1121-2210-timp tr tamb glock hp str)
Hawkes & Son (piano conductor & parts) 1939); now hire Boosey & Hawkes. (No 2 previously pub arr pf or orch Winthrop Rogers 1927)
MS Boosey & Hawkes. *See also* 145
Timing 6½' (set) 2½' (no 2)

42 **[Five] Entr'actes** *see* [The] Two Hunchbacks
Etude Rhapsodique, for piano (Nov 1906)
Unpublished; MS Parry Room

43 **Evening Primrose** (2-part song), wds-John Clare
OUP 1923 (The *Oxford Choral Songs*, no 102)

44 **Fair Daffodils** — song for voice & piano, wds-Herrick (April 1905)
Winthrop Rogers 1919; Boosey & Hawkes

45 **[The] Fairy Ring** — 3-part song with piano accompaniment
OUP 1923 (The *Oxford Choral Songs*, no 202)

46 **[A] Fairy Tale:** suite for piano (1917)
No 1 *The Princess* (Augener 1918); no 2 *The Ogre*; no 3 *The Spell* (Augener 1927); no 4 *The Prince.* (Augener 1918; Stainer & Bell)

47 **Far, Far From Each Other** — song for voice & piano with viola obbligato, wds-Matthew Arnold (1906)
Unpublished
Finale *see* Suite for Strings
Fireflies *see* Characteristic Pieces — 4

48 **Fly Home My Thoughts** — song for voice & piano or orchestra (Midsummer 1904)
Voice & piano score, no orchestral score or parts

49 [Two] **Folk Songs** *see* [Two] Old English Songs
Gargoyle (for piano) (Friston, July 1928)
Unpublished; MS Parry Room

50 **For God and King and Right** (unison song with piano or orchestra), wds-V Mason
Schirmer (vocal score) 1916; Boosey & Hawkes. Orchestral version on hire from Boosey & Hawkes (2+1, 222-4220-timp sd bd cym str)
Timing 11'
Fragrance *see* Characteristic Pieces — 2
Galliarde *see* [The] Pageant of London
Gavotte *see* [Three] Miniature Pastorals, set 1 no 2

51 **Goldenhair** (*Lean out of the window*) — song for voice & piano, wds-James Joyce (Oct 29 1925)
Chappell 1925
MS destroyed in Chappell's 1964 fire. Another Holograph, from the collection of Miss Margery Foss, is now in the Parry Room but is uncatalogued

52 **Golden Slumbers** (3-part song, unaccompanied), wds-T Dekker
Augener 1923

53 **Gondoliera** (for violin & piano)
Augener 1915

54 **Go Not, Happy Day** — song for voice & piano or arr voice & orch., wds-Tennyson (1903)
Published in *The Vocalist*, no 42 (1905). Low voice in G, high voice in A: Winthrop Rogers; Boosey & Hawkes. Orchestral version on hire (high voice, in A only) from Boosey & Hawkes (arr Wurmser), Voice & strings, timing 1' 25"; also arr G Williams, voice, harp & strings

55 [The] **Graceful Swaying Wattle** (2-part song with piano or strings), wds-V Mason
Schirmer 1916; Boosey & Hawkes. Orchestral version (strings) on hire from Boosey & Hawkes
Timing 2'

56 **Graziella** (for piano)
Winthrop Rogers 1927; Boosey & Hawkes
MS Boosey & Hawkes

57 [The] **Hag** — song for baritone & orchestra, wds-Herrick (18 June 1902)
Unpublished
Full score & parts (2+1, 222-4231-timp cym bd str), Parry Room

58 **Happy South** (piano)
Unpublished
MS Boosey & Hawkes

59 **Harebell and Pansy** — unfinished song for voice & orchestra (1905)
Incomplete piano & voice score, Parry Room

Heart's Ease see [Three] Lyrics

[The] **Hedgerow** see [Three] Lyrics — 3

60 **Hence Care** — (3-part song)
Augener 1923

61 **Hidden Fires** (for piano) c 1925
Winthrop Rogers 1927; Boosey & Hawkes
MS Boosey & Hawkes

Hornpipe see [Three] Miniature Pastorals set 3 no 8

62 [The] **Hour Glass** — three piece for piano: no 1 *Dusk*; no 2 *The Dew Fairy*; no 3 *The Midnight Tide*
Augener 1920; Stainer & Bell

Hunchback see [The] Two Hunchbacks

63 [Three] **Idylls for string quartet** (1906)
Augener (score & parts) 1911
The second is the source of the theme in Benjamin Britten's *Variations on a Theme of Frank Bridge*

64 **If I Could Choose** — song for voice & piano, wds-T Ashe
Keith Prowse 1902

65 [Three] **Improvisations for piano (left hand):** no 1 *At Dawn*; no 2 *A Vigil*; no 3 *A Revel*
Winthrop Rogers 1919; Boosey & Hawkes

66 **In Autumn** — 2 pieces for piano: no 1 *Retrospect*; no 2 *Through the Eaves* (1924)
Augener 1925; no 1 Galliard; Stainer & Bell

67 **Incidental music for an unidentified play (for piano)**
MS Parry Room

68 **In Memoriam C.H.H.P.** [i.e. **Sir Hubert Parry**] (for organ) 15 Oct 1918
Deane & Sons, 1924, (not in BM)
MS Parry Room

Intermezzo see Threads

Intermezzo *see* [Three] Miniature pastorals set 2 no 5

69 **In the Shop, Act II** (piano, 4-hands), ?ballet music (nd)
   MS Benjamin Britten

70 **Into Her Keeping** (*Now that my love lies sleeping*) — song for voice & piano, wds-H D Lowry (4 May 1919)
   Winthrop Rogers 1919; Boosey & Hawkes
   I Praise the Tender Flower *see* [Two] Songs

71 **[An] Irish Melody** (The Londonderry Air) 1908
   Originated as part of a joint string quartet, 'Hambourg' Quartet, the remaining movements being by Harty, Davies & Eric Coates
   Published for string quartet (parts) Augener 1915; (miniature score) Augener 1924: for string orchestra (miniature score) Augener 1939

72 **Isabella,** symphonic poem after Keats (for orchestra) 1907
   Unpublished
   MS score & parts (Parry Room); (3(1), +1, 2+1, 2+1—42+2,3,1-timp sd tri bd cym hp (2 copies provided) str)
   First performance Queen's Hall 3 Oct 1907

73 **Isobel** (*What is the sorrow of the wind*) — song for voice & piano, wds-Digby Goddard-Fenwick (Sept 1912)
   Chappell 1913
   MS destroyed in Chappell's 1964 fire
   Orchestrated G Stacey (strings & pf) in A min, on hire from Chappell

74 **Journey's End** (*What will they give me when journey's done?*) — song for voice & piano, wds-Humbert Wolfe (21 Nov 1925)
   Augener 1926. Reissued as (Four) Songs — 4, *qv*

74 **Lament** (*Fall now my cold thoughts*) — song for voice & piano (Midsummer 1904)
   Unpublished
   May have been intended for orchestration but no score has been found

76 **Lament for string orchestra (or piano)** 1915
   Goodwin & Tabb (full score & parts) 1915; Goodwin & Tabb (piano solo) 1915; Curwen; materials available on hire from Faber Music
   Timing 5′ 30-7′ 00″
   [Une] Lamantatione d'Amour *see* Romance 'Une Lamentatione d'Amour

77 **Lantido Dilly** (for 3-part voices)
   Winthrop Rogers 1920 ('School Songs'); Boosey & Hawkes

78 **[The] Last Invocation** (*At the last tenderly*) — song for voice & piano (23 Sept 1918), wds-Walt Whitman
   Winthrop Rogers 1919; Boosey & Hawkes

79 **Lay a Garland** (2-part vocal canon with accompaniment), wds-Beaumont & Fletcher
Winthrop Rogers 1919; Boosey & Hawkes
80 **Lean Close Thy Cheek** — song for voice & piano, wds-Heine (10 April 1905)
Unpublished
81 **Life** (*The air with balmy fragrancy*) — song for voice & piano (?1904)
Unpublished
82 [A] **Litany** (for 3-part voices, accompaniment ad lib), wds-P Fletcher
Winthrop Rogers 1919 ('School Songs'); Boosey & Hawkes
[The] **Londonderry Air** *see* [An] Irish Melody
83 **Love** (*Through life's long day and passion's pain*) — song for voice & piano (7 Sept 1904)
Unpublished
84 **Love is a Rose** — song for voice & piano (31 Dec 1907), wds-Leak Durand
Unpublished
Love Went a Riding *see* [Two] Songs — 2
85 **Lullaby** (for 3-part voices & accommpaniment), wds-V Mason
Schirmer 1916 (voices & piano); Boosey & Hawkes; orchestral version (strings) on hire from Boosey & Hawkes
Timing 2′
Lullaby *see* Short Pieces for Violin & Piano — 3
86 [Four] **Lyrics:** No 1 *Dawn and Evening*; no 2 *E'en as a Lovely Flower*; no 3 *The Violets Blue*; no 4 *All Things That We Clasp*
No 1, originally translated beginning *Rising when the dawn still faint is* (28 July 1903), published *The Vocalist* no 43 (1905), translation described as being by 'C A'. Revised April 1905 beginning *Dawn awakening hears my calling*, translated by Francis Heuffer, published Boosey & Co 1916 in collected album of 'Four Lyrics'; published separately Boosey & Hawkes. *No 2*: translated by Kate Freiligrath Kroeker (20 Aug 1903), published *The Vocalist* no 43 (1905). Reissued in album of 'Four Lyrics', Boosey & Co 1916; published separately (low- & high-voice versions) Boosey & Hawkes. *No 3*: translated James Thomson after Heine (5 Sept 1906), published in album of 'Four Lyrics', Boosey & Co 1916; published separately Boosey & Hawkes (also arr string quartet — hire Boosey & Hawkes). *No 4*: translated Emma Lazarus after Heine (1907), published in album of 'Four Songs', Boosey & Co 1916; published separately Boosey & Hawkes. *Nos 1 & 2* also in orchestral version. No 2 (1121-2000-hp str) on hire from Boosey & Hawkes

87 **[Three] Lyrics** (for piano): no 1 *Heart's Ease* (26 April 1921); no 2 *Dainty Rogue* (1922); no 3 *The Hedgerow* (1924)
Augener 1922, 1925; Stainer & Bell
MS of no 1: Library of Congress

88 **Mantle of Blue** (*O men from the fields*) — song for high voice & piano or high voice & orchestra, wds-Padraic Colum (March 1918)
Winthrop Rogers 1919; Boosey & Hawkes; orchestral version on hire from Boosey & Hawkes (2222-2000-hp str)
Timing 3' 00"

March *see* Coronation March

March *see* [The] Pageant of London

March Militaire *see* [Three] Miniature Pastorals, set 3 no 9

Meditation (for cello and piano), *arrangement of short pieces for violin & piano qv*

89 **Mélodie for violin & piano** (or cello & piano)
Goodwin & Tabb 1911 (Boston, The BF Wood Music Co 1911)

90 **[A] Merry, Merry Xmas** (variations on *Good King Wenceslas* for piano clarinet, oboe & trombone)
Unpublished
MS Library of Congress

[The Midnight Tide *see* [The] Hour Glass — 3

91 **Three] Miniatures** (for violin, cello & Piano): 3 sets (1906-1907)
Goodwin & Tabb (sets 1 & 2) 1909; Goodwin & Tabb (set 3) 1915
Contents: Set 1, no 1 *Minuet*, no 2 *Gavotte*, no 3 *Allegretto*. Set 2, no 4 *Romance*, no 5 *Intermezzo*, no 6 *Saltarello*. Set 3, no 7 *Valse russe*, no 8 *Hornpipe*, no 9 *Marche Militaire*

92 **[Three] Miniature pastorals (for piano):** 2 sets
Winthrop Rogers (set 1) 1917; Winthrop Rogers (set 2) 1921; Boosey & Hawkes
see also 120

93 **Minuet, for organ** (1939)
Curwen 1940

Minuet *see* [Three] Miniature pastorals set 1 no 1

Minuet *see* [Three] Piano pieces — 2

Minuet *see* [The] Pageant of London

94 **Moderato in E minor for Piano** (Cardigan Sept 5 1903)
Unpublished
MS Parry Room

Moonlight *see* [The] Sea

95 **[Three] Morceaux d'Orchestre:** no 1 *Chant de Tristesse* (April 1902); no 2 *Chant d'Esperance* (11 April 1902, scored Aug 1902); no 3 *Chant de Gaieté* (9 Sept 1902)

Unpublished (1121-02+1,10-cym hp str)
MS fullscore: Parry Room

96 **Morning Song** (for cello & piano)
Winthrop Rogers 1919; Boosey & Hawkes

97 **Moto Perpetuo** (for violin & piano)
Goodwin & Tabb 1911; Augener 1925

98 **(Two) Movements for string quartet:** no 1 *Pizzicati*; no 2 *Adagio* (1904)
An example of an early Bridge work intended for the 'Chips' quartet, usually of a humorous nature (1 includes *The Rag* — short score (sketch) & pts of introduction, then 2 variations on *Old Folkes at Home* (1906) — introduction quotes Beethoven op 18 no 1 and Fifth Symphony)

99 **Music, When Soft Voices Die** — song for voice & piano (11 Nov 1903) or for voice & piano with viola obliggato (11 Jan 1907), wds-Shelley
Both versions unpublished

100 **My Pent-up Tears** — song for voice & piano (27 Dec 1906)
Unpublished
Nicoletta *see* Vignettes de Dance

101 **Night Lies on the Silent Highways** — song for voice & piano, wds-Heine, translated by Kate Freiligrath Kroeker (12 Jan 1904)
Unpublished
Nocturne *see* Divertimenti
Nocturne *see* Suite for Strings

102 **Norse Legend** (for orchestra, or piano, or violin & piano) 1905
Hawkes & Son 1939 (piano conductor & parts — 1121-2210-timp hp str); Winthrop Rogers (violin & piano) 1918; Boosey & Hawkes 1939
Timing 4' 00" -4' 30"

103 **[Three] Noveletten** (for string quartet) 1906
Augener (min score & string parts) 1915; (min score 1924)
[The] Ogre *see* [A] Fairy Tale-Suite

104 **[Two] Old English Songs:** no 1 *Sally in Our Alley*; no 2 *Cherry Ripe* (arranged for piano solo, piano duet, string quartet or string orchestra with ad lib double bass part) 1916
Schirmer (piano duet) 1916; Schirmer (score) 1916; Winthrop Rogers (piano solo); Boosey & Hawkes. String parts & score available on hire from Boosey & Hawkes
Timing 7' 35" 2: 3' 40"
Old Folkes at Home *see* [Two] Movements for String Quartet
[The] Open Air *see* [Two] Poems for Orchestra — 1

105 **Oration — concerto elegiaco** (for cello & orchestra) ('sketch 25 March 1930; score 9 May 1930; Epilogue 25 June 1930')

Unpublished; a copy orchestral score by J Walker is in the Parry Room. Score & parts (2 (1) 222-4231-timp sd tr hp str) on hire from Faber Music
Timing 28
First performance — Broadcasting House, F Hooton/orch F Bridge 16 Jan 1936

106 [First Book of] Organ Pieces (1905): no 1 *Allegro Grazioso*; no 2 *Allegro Commodo*; no 3 *Allegro Marziale*
Winthrop Rogers 1917; Boosey & Hawkes

107 [Second Book of] Organ Pieces: no 1 *Andante con moto*; no 2 *Andantino*; no 3 *Allegro ben moderato*
Boosey & Hawkes 1914 (no 3 originally published in *The Organ Loft*, Book 105, 1901)

108 [Three] Organ Pieces: no 1 *Andante Moderato in C minor*; no 2 *Adagio in E major*; no 3 *Allegro con spirito in Bb major* (a collection of pieces previously published B7, B1, B4)
Novello 196?

109 O That It Were So (*It sometimes comes into my head*) — song for voice & piano or voice & orchestra, wds-Walter Savage Landor (?1913)
Chappell (voice & piano) 1913 (orch version formerly on hire from Chappell but survives at BBC, in Eb, B & Bb (1121-220-perc str) in Ab (1121-221-perc-pf-str) in D & Bb — arr Stacey: str & pf)
MS destroyed in Chappell's 1964 fire

110 [The] Pageant of London (c 1911)
No music for this event has been traced, but the *Musical Times* (June 1911, p 384) reports that Bridge supplied the following music for wind band: *Solemn March, March, Minuet, Pavane* and *Galliarde* [sic]

111 Pan's Holiday (2-part song), wds-J Shirley
OUP 1923 (*Oxford Choral Songs* no 103)
Pavane *see* [The] Pageant of London

112 Pensées Fugitives (1) for piano (Summer 1902)
Unpublished
MS Parry Room

113 Pensiero (for viola & piano)
Stainer & Bell 1908 (*Lionel Tertis' Viola Library* — no 1)
See also 125 no 1

114 Peter Piper (unaccompanied 3-part song)
Schirmer 1916; Boosey & Hawkes
Phantasie *see also* Phantasy

115 **Phantasie in C minor** (for violin, cello, piano) [ie Piano Trio no 1] (1907)
Novello (1909)

116 **Phantasie for String Quartet in F sharp minor** (6 May 1901-21 July 1901)
Novello for the Company of Musicians 1906 (parts only)
MS score & parts (Parry Room)
First performed RCM 4 Dec 1901

117 **Phantasm** — rhapsody for piano & orchestra (1931)
Augener (2-piano reduction)
MS score & parts available from Stainer & Bell (2(1)222-4231-timp tr cym tam-tam str)
Timing 25' 00"

118 **Phantasy in F sharp minor** (for piano quartet) 2 June 1910
Goodwin & Tabb (score & parts) 1911 (*Cobbett Series no 1*); reissued Augener 1920
MS score & parts (Parry Room)

119 [Three] **Piano Pieces:** no 1 *Columbine*; no 2 *Minuet*; no 3 *Romance*
Augener 1913; Stainer & Bell

120 [Four] **Piano Pieces** (21-28 April 1921)
Unpublished
MS Parry Room
(Hindmarsh suggests 1, 2 & 3 intended as 3rd set of Miniature Pastorals)

Piano Quartet *see* Phantasie for piano quartet

121 **Piano Quintet** (for piano, 2 violins, viola & cello) 1904-1912
Augener (piano score & parts) 1919

122 **Piano Sonata** (1921-1924)
Augener 1925; Stainer & Bell
First performance: Myra Hess, Wigmore Hall 15 Oct 1925

Piano Trio no 1 *see* Phantasie in C minor

123 **Piano Trio no 2** (for violin, cello & piano) 1929
Published Augener (piano score & parts) 1930
Timing 28' 30"
MS Library of Congress

124 [Two] **Pieces for Two Violas**
No final copy of this work has been found, although an incomplete sketch is preserved at the Parry Room. The work is known to exist from the list of viola works in Lionel Tertis' *My Viola & I* (Elek 1975) and from a notice in the *Musical Times* (April 1912 p 259)

125   **[Two] Pieces for viola & piano** (1905): no 1 [1st version of] *Pensiero* (23 March 1905) see also 113; no 2 unfinished, completed by Paul Hindmarsh
Unpublished
MS Parry Room
Pizzicati *see* [Two] Movements for String Quartet
Poem *see* Dance Poem

126   **[Two] Poems for Orchestra** — after Richard Jefferies (1915): no 1 *The Open Air*; no 2 *The Story of My Heart* (piano score, Parry Room, is untitled and undated for no 1)
Augener (full score and min score) 1923; score & parts on hire (Stainer & Bell: No 1: 2222-4000-timp hp str. No 2: 2+1222-4231-timp tr glock cymb sd hp str.
Timing 10′ 00″-11′ 15″

127   **[Three] Poems for piano** (1913-1915): no 1 *Solitude*; no 2 *Ecstacy*; no 3 *Sunset*
Augener 1915; Stainer & Bell

128   **[A] Prayer for chorus & orchestra,** wds-Thomas a Kempis (1916)
Augener (vocal score) 1918; Augener (string parts) 1919; (wind parts arranged organ) Augener 1925; score & parts on hire (Stainer & Bell: 2+1,2,2,2-4431-timp bd cym str)
Timing: 20′ 30″

Prelude *see* Divertimenti — 1
Prelude *see* Suite for Strings — 1

129   **Prelude for organ** (1939)
Curwen 1940

130   **[The] Primrose** — a song for voice & piano, wds-Herrick
Keith Prowse 1902

[The] Prince *see* [A] Fairy Tale-suite — 4
[The] Princess *see* [A] Fairy Tale-suite — 1

131   **Processional, for organ** (1939)
Curwen 1940

Quartet for strings *see* String Quartet
Quintet for piano & strings *see* Piano Quintet
[The] Rag *see* [Two] Movements for String Quartet

132   **Rebus** — overture (for orchestra) 1940
Unpublished
MS, 2 scores Boosey & Hawkes. Copyist's score & parts available on hire from Boosey & Hawkes (3(1), 2+1, 2+1, 2+1-4331-tim sd bd cym tr hp str)
Timing 8′ 00″-9′ 00″
First performance LPO/Wood 23 Feb 1941

133 **Rhapsody** (for 2 violins & viola) March 1928
Faber Music (score & parts) (F 0006) 1965
MS (Score) Parry Room; set of parts marked 'version 2' (Parry Room)

134 **Romance** — **'Une Lamentatione D'Amour'** (for violin & piano) Aug 17 1900
Unpublished
MS Parry Room (but uncatalogued)
Romance see [Three] Miniature pastorals set 2 no 4

135 **Romance** see [Three] Piano pieces — 3
Romanze (for violin & piano) Xmas 1904
'A German Parody over FB's name' — Hindmarsh
Unpublished
MS Parry Room (uncatalogued)
Rosemary (for piano or orchestra) see [Three] Sketches (for piano) — 2 and [Two] Entr'actes (for orchestra)
Sally in Our Alley see [Two] Old English Folksongs

136 **Saltarello** see [Three] Miniature pastorals set 2 no 6
Scherzetto (for cello & piano) (c 1902)
Unpublished
MS Parry Room

137 **Scherzetto** see Divertimenti — 3
Scherzettino (for piano) pre-1904
Unpublished
MS Parry Room

138 **Scherzo Phantastick** for string quartet (8 July 1901)
Score plus 4 parts (Parry Room)
Unpublished
Davies observes: 'A humourous work played by the 'Chips' quartet

139 **[The] Sea** — suite for orchestra: no 1 *Seascape*; no 2 *Seafoam*; no 3 *Moonlight*; no 4 *Storm* (1910-1911)
Stainer & Bell (full score) 1920 (Carnegie Collection of British Music). Score & parts on hire from Stainer & Bell (3(1),2+1,2+1, 2+1-4331-timp tr sd cym bd hp str)
Timing 19' 15"-23' 15"
In his 78rpm recording Bridge alters the end of the storm; no ms of this version has been found
First performance, London (Henry Wood) 24 Sept 1912
Seafoam see [The] Sea
[A] Sea Idyll see [Two] Solos for the piano — 1
Seascape see [The] Sea

140 **Serenade** [for orchestra]
Reid (piano); available on hire (PC & 1121-2210-timp tr hp str) Reid, later Chappell, now survives at BBC

141 **Serenade** (for violin & piano or cello & piano or piano solo)
Bunz (violin or cello & piano) 1906; Bunz (piano) 1910

142 **Sextet for strings** (2 violins, 2 violas, 2 celli) 1906-1912
Augener (score & parts) 1920

143 **[Four] Short Pieces for Violin & Piano:** no 1 *Meditation*; no 2 *Spring Song*; no 3 *Lullaby*; no 4 *Country Dance*
Augener 1912 (nos 1 & 2 also issued for cello & piano, 1912)
Sir Roger de Coverley *see* [A] Christmas Dance

144 **Sister Awake!** (2-part song with accompaniment), wds-T Bateson
Winthrop Rogers 1919; Boosey & Hawkes

145 **[Three] Sketches for the pianoforte** (1906): no 1 *April*; no 2 *Rosemary*; no 3 *Valse Capriccieuse* (no 1 later published by Winthrop Rogers)
Schirmer 1915; Boosey & Hawkes
Timing (set) 7' 05" 2: 2' 45"
No 2 orchestrated as no 2 of [Two] Entr'actes, published as piano conductor, Hawkes & sons 1939, see 41

146 **So Early in the Morning** (*I cling and swing on a branch*) — song for voice & piano, wds-James Stephens (Feb 1918)
Winthrop Rogers 1918; Boosey & Hawkes
Solemn March *see* [The] Pageant of London
Solitude *see* [Three] Poems

147 **[Two] Solos for the Piano:** no 1 [A] *Sea Idyll*; no 2 *Capriccioin F sharp minor* (1902)
Houghton & Co 1906; no 1 reissued Augener 1917; Stainer & Bell

148 **[Two] Songs for tenor & piano or tenor & orchestra,** wds-Mary E Coleridge: no 1 *Where She Lies Asleep* (April 1914); no 2 *Love Went a Riding* (5 May 1914)
Schirmer 1916; Winthrop Rogers 1918; Boosey & Hawkes (no 2) low voice in E, high voice in Gb; (no 2) French version by Lilian Fearn with simplified accompaniment (Boosey & Hawkes *Melodies Anglaises* 1946). Orchestral versions available on hire from Boosey & Hawkes: no 1 2332-4000-hp str; no 2 (in E or Gb) 2+1,2+1,3(2), 2-4(or 2)231(or 0)-timp glock tr cym hp str)
Timing 3' each song

149 **[Two] Songs [for high] baritone & orchestra,** wds-Robert Bridges: no1 *I Praise the Tender Flower* (Oct 1905, scored 2 Jan 1906); no 2 *Thou Didst Delight my Eyes* (scored 20 Jan 1906)
Unpublished

Score, voice & piano sketches & 23 parts (2+1,2,2,2 4221 timp str) (Parry Room)

150 **[Three] Songs for voice & piano or voice & orchestra** (Rubindranath Tagore): no 1 *Day After Day* (1922); no 2 *Speak To Me My Love* (Oct 1924); no 3 *Dweller in My Deathless Dreams* (1 June 1925)
Augener (1 & 2) 1925; Augener (no 3) 1926 (Reprinted in [Four] Songs *qv*). Orchestral versions of 1 (1122-1000 hp str) and 2 (2222-2000 hp str) available on hire from Stainer & Bell
MS of no 3: Library of Congress
[Four] Songs by Frank Bridge
A reprinted collection of [Three] Songs (Tagore) and *Journey's End* (Humbert Wolfe), with an introduction by Peter J Pirie, Galliard 1974

151 **So Perverse** — song for voice & piano, wds-Bridges (1905)
Published in *The Vocalist* (1905); Schirmer 1916; Boosey & Hawkes

152 **Souvenir** (for violin & piano)
Winthrop Rogers 1919; Boosey & Hawkes
Speak to Me, My Love *see* [Three] Songs (Tagore)
[The] Spell *see* [A] Fairy Tale-suite for piano — 3

153 **[A] Spring Song** (unison song), wds-M Howitt
OUP 1923 (*The Oxford Choral Songs* — no 2)
Spring Song (for violin or cello & piano) *see* Short Pieces for Violin & Piano — 2
Storm *see* [The] Sea — 4
[The] Story of My Heart *see* [Two] Poems for Orchestra

154 **Strew No More Red Roses** — song for voice & piano, wds-Matthew Arnold (10 April 1913)
Winthrop Rogers 1917; Boosey & Hawkes

155 **String Quartet in E minor (No 1) 'Bologna'** (1906)
Avison Edition (score & parts); Cary & Co 1916; Augener (Parts) 1920

156 **String Quartet in G minor (No 2)** (1915)
Novello (score) 1916 (The Cobbett Prize-winner for 1915)

157 **String Quartet no 3** (17 May 1926)
Augener (miniature score & parts) 1928; miniature score reissued Galliard c 1972
MS Parry Room (another Holograph is in the Library of Congress)
First performance Washington 17 Sept 1927

158 **String Quartet no 4** (6 Nov 1937)
Augener (miniature score & parts) 1939; miniature score reissued Galliard c 1972

MS Library of Congress
String Sextet see sextet for strings

159 **Suite for String Orchestra** (1908); no 1 *Prelude*; no 2 *Intermezzo*; no 3 *Nocturne*, no 4 *Finale*
Goodwin & Tabb (full score) 1920; Curwen; materials available on hire from Faber Music
Timing 21' 00" -24' 00"

160 **Summer** — tone poem (for orchestra) (sketch July 1914, score 11 April 1915)
Augener (full score) 1923; score & parts on hire from Stainer & Bell (2(1),222-2200-timp perc celesta hp str)
MS full score, Parry Room
Timing 9' 55" -12' 00"
First performance conducted by Bridge 13 March 1916
Sunset see [Three] Poems — 3

161 **Symphonic Poem** (for orchestra) 18 Oct 1903
Unpublished
Full score & parts Parry Room (3(1),2+1,22-4231-timp cym str)
First performed 20 May 1904, St James Hall, at a Patron Fund concert

162 **Symphony** (for strings — unfinished) Nov/Dec 1940, 10 Jan 1941
Unpublished
Full score (357 bars) of opening movement, *Allegro Moderato*, Parry Room

163 **Tears, Idle Tears** — song for voice & piano, wds-Tennyson (1905)
Unpublished

164 **Theme in Eb minor** (for piano)
Unpublished
Unfinished MS Parry Room
Thou Didst Delight My Eyes (song) see [Two] Songs

165 **Threads** — incidental music to a play by Frank Stayton (1921)
Intermezzi (piano or orchestra): no 1 *Andante molto moderato e tranquillo*; no 2 *Tempo di Valse*
Hawkes & Son (piano conductor & orchestral parts) 1939; Boosey & Hawkes (pc-1121-2210-timp perc hp str)
Timing 3' 00", 4' 30" respectively

166 **There is a Willow Grows Aslant a Brook** — impressions for small orchestra (1928)
Augener (score & parts) 1928; Augener (miniature score) 1933. Score & parts available on hire from Stainer & Bell (1121-1000-hp-str)
Timing 9' 15" -10' 00"

167 **Though Didst Delight My Eyes** — song for high baritone voice & piano or voice & orchestra, wds-Robert Bridges (?Oct 1905, scored 20 Jan 1906)
Unpublished
Through the Eaves *see* In Autumn — 2
168 **Thy Hand in Mine** — song for voice & piano or voice & orchestra, wds-Mary Coleridge (10 Feb 1917)
Winthrop Rogers 1917; Boosey & Hawkes Orchestral version available on hire from Boosey & Hawkes (2222-2200 hp str)
MS of voice & orchestra version Boosey & Hawkes
Timing 2' 00"
169 **'Tis But A Week** — song for voice & piano, wds-Gerald Gould (1 June 1919)
Winthrop Rogers 1919; Boosey & Hawkes (medium voice in B)
170 **Todessehnsucht (Come Sweet Death)** auf dem Schemellischen Gesangbuch [of] J S Bach, arranged Frank Bridge for string orchestra (13 Feb 1936) — an arrangement for strings of a piano piece in the *Harriet Cohen Book*, OUP 1932
MS Benjamin Britten
171 **To You in France** — song for voice & piano
Incomplete sketches are preserved in the Parry Room
Trio for violin, viola & piano *see Piano Trio*
Trio for 2 violins & viola *see* Rhapsody
172 **[The] Turtle's Retort** (for piano)
Published under the pseudonym of John L Moore, Boosey & Hawkes
173 **[The] Two Hunchbacks** (play by Emile Cammaerts) 1908
[Five] Entr'actes
Unpublished; full score & 20 orchestral parts (3222-4231 hp str), Parry Room
Valse Capriceuse *see* [Three] Sketches — 3
174 **Valse Intermezzo a cordes** (22 Aug 1902)
Unpublished; full score & 6 parts Parry Room
Valse Russe *see* [Three] Miniature pastorals set 3 no 7
175 **Variations on 'Cadet Rouselle'** (joint variations with Bax, Ireland & Goossens)
Chester (voice & piano) 1920; full orchestral score (orch Goossens, Dec 1930); Chester 1931 (2221-2100-sd tr glock xyl tub bells cym hp timp str)
[A] **Vigil** *see* Improvisations for piano (left hand) — 2
176 **Vignettes de Dance** (for small orchestra) (1925-1940): no 1 *Nicoletta*; no 2

Zoraida; no 3 *Carmelita*
Unpublished; score & parts available on hire from Boosey & Hawkes (1121-2210-timp tr cym tamb cast sd hp str)
Timing 10'
First performance BBC Glasgow 12 May 1941
A piano score of *En Fête* (Nov 16 1925) appears as no 4 in the piano sketch MS at the Parry Room
[The] **Violets Blue** *see* [Four] Lyrics — 3

177 **Violin Sonata** (1904)
Unfinished; unpublished
MS (1st movement, 13 April 1904; 2nd movement unfinished): Parry Room

178 **Violin Sonata** (21 Nov 1932)
Augener 1933
MS Library of Congress
First performed Wigmore Hall 18 Jan 1934
Water Nymphs (for piano) *see* Characteristic Pieces — 1

179 **What Shall I Your True Love Tell** — song for voice & piano, wds-Francis Thompson (31 May 1919)
Winthrop Rogers 1919; Boosey & Hawkes

180 **When Most I Wink** (Sonnet) — song for voice & piano, wds-Shakespeare (8 April 1901)
Unpublished

181 **When You Are Old** — song for voice & piano, wds-W B Yeats (25 Jan 1919)
Chappell 1920
MS destroyed in Chappell's 1964 fire

182 **Where'er My Bitter Teardrops Fall** — song for voice & piano, wds-Heine translated by J E Wallis (30 July 1903)
Unpublished

183 **Where It Is That Our Soul Doth Go** — song for voice & piano with viola obliggato, wds-Heine translated by J E Wallis (Christmas 1906)
Unpublished
Where She Lies Asleep *see* [Two] Songs

184 **Winter Pastoral** (for piano)
Augener 1928; Galliard
Zoraida *see* Vignettes de Dance

ARRANGEMENTS

Bach (J S): Komm Süsser Tod *see* Todessehnsucht *in main sequence*
185 **Corelli (A):** Twelve Grand Concerts: no VIII ('Christmas Concerto'), edited by Frank Bridge (1911)
186 **Hurlstone (W Y)** Sonata in D Major — *Adagio Lamentoso* only, transcribed by Frank Bridge (1909)
Easter Hymn *see* main sequence
Variations on 'Cadet Rousselle' (by Bridge, Bax, Goossens & Ireland) for voice & piano (Chester 1920), for orchestra (orch Goossens) Chester 1931 *see* main sequence

WORKS BY CATEGORY

(numbers as in the list of works on previous pages)

PIANO

Solo
9, 11, 15, 18, 31, 39, 42, 46, 49, 56, 58, 61, 62, 65, 66, 76, 87, 92, 94. 102, 104, 112, 119, 120, 122, 127, 137, 140, 141, 145, 147, 164, 165, 172, 184

Duet
104

With orchestra
117

With violin, cello
91, 115, 123

With violin, viola, cello
118

With 2 violins, viola, cello
121

With clarinet, oboe and trombone
90

ORGAN
1, 4, 6, 7, 8, 37, 68, 93, 106, 107, 108, 129, 131

VIOLIN

With piano
5, 11, 23, 26, 53, 89, 97, 102, 134, 136, 141, 143, 152, 177, 178

With orchestra
11

2 violins and viola
133

CELLO
With piano
11, 16, 17, 26, 38, 89, 96, 136, 141, 143

With orchestra
105

VIOLA
With piano
3, 113, 124, 125

2 violas
124

With 2 violins
133

STRING QUARTET
19, 37, 63, 71, 86, 98, 103, 104, 116, 138, 155, 156, 157, 158

PIANO TRIO (piano, violin, cello)
91, 115, 123

PIANO QUARTET (piano, violin, viola, cello)
118

PIANO QUINTET (piano, 2 violins, viola, cello)
121

STRING SEXTET (2 violins, 2 violas, 2 cello)
142

WIND
34, 110

FLUTE
37

BELLS
37

CLARINET
90

OBOE
90

TROMBONE
90

ORCHESTRA
11 (with violin), 19 (strings), 23, 24, 27, 28, 35, 40, 41 (small), 71 (strings), 72, 76 (strings), 95, 102, 104 (strings), 105 (with cello), 117 (with piano), 126, 129 (with chorus), 132, 139, 140, 145, 159 (strings), 160, 161, 162 (strings), 165, 166 (small), 170 (strings), 173, 176 (small)

OPERA
20

BALLET
69

VOCAL

Songs with piano
2, 12, 13, 14, 21, 25, 29, 30, 32, 33, 36, 44, 47, 48, 51, 54, 57, 64, 70, 73, 74, 75, 78, 80, 81, 83, 84, 86, 88, 99, 100, 101, 109, 130, 146, 148, 150, 151, 154, 163, 167, 168, 169, 171, 175, 179, 180, 181, 182, 183

Songs with orchestra
2, 12, 14, 54, 69, 73, 86, 88, 109, 148, 149, 150, 167

Choral
10 (SATB), 36 (mixed), 43 (2-part), 45 (3-part), 50 (unison), 52 (3-part), 55 (2-part, also with strings), 60 (3-part), 77 (3-part), 79 (2-part), 82 (3-part), 85 (3-part, also with strings), 111 (2-part), 114 (3-part), 153 (unison)

BIBLIOGRAPHY

JOHN BISHOP

Books, encyclopaedias, newspapers and periodical articles, record sleeves, published in Britain unless otherwise named.

Antcliffe, Herbert. 'Frank Bridge', *Sackbut* (May 1925), 286.
Abraham, Gerald. 'Frank Bridge', *Die Musik in Geschichte und Gegenwart*, hrsgb. Friedrich Blume (Kassel u. Basel: Barenreiter, 1952), 11, 319.
Bishop, John. Sleeve-notes for Pearl SHE 513/4 (1974).
  'Frank Bridge', *Composer* (Spring 1976).
Britten, Benjamin. 'Britten Looking Back', *Musical America*, LXXXIV (February 1964). 4.
Bye, Frederick. *Strad*, XLI (1930), 136.
Cobbett, W W, ed. Cobbett's Cyclopaedic Survey of Chamber Music. (Oxford University Press, 1929, 1963).
Current Biography: Who News and Why. 1941 edition (New York: H W Wilson, 1941).
Demuth, Norman. 'Composers in Sussex', *Sussex Life* (April 1968).
Douglas, D. 'Sussex Musicians', *Sussex County Magazine* (March 1941), 99.
Dunhill. Thomas F. 'Frank Bridge's New Trio', *Monthly Musical Record*, LX (April 1, 1930), 104.
Evans, Edwin. 'Modern British Composers: I — Frank Bridge', *Musical Times*, LX (February 1919), 55.
  'In Memoriam: Frank Bridge and Sir Hamilton Harty', *Music Review*, II (1941), 159.
  'Frank Bridge', Grove's Dictionary of Music and Musicians, 5th ed. (Macmillan, 1954), I, 933.
Ewen, David, ed. Composers of Today, 2nd ed. (New York: H W Wilson, 1936).
Furley, Mabel McDonough. *Musical America*, XXXIX (November 17, 1923), 33.
Goddard, Scott. 'Frank Bridge', *Monthly Musical Record*, LXXI (1941), 59.
Henderson, Robert. 'Bridge and Britten', *Musical Times*, CVIII (June 1967), 524.
Holbrooke, Joseph. Contemporary British Composers (Palmer, 1925).
Howells, Herbert. 'Frank Bridge', *Music and Letters,* XXII (1941), 208.
Hull, A E. 'The Neo-British School', *Monthly Musical Record*, Ll (1921), 52.

'A.J.' *Opera*, XVII (February 1966). 164.

James, Ivor. 'Obituary: Frank Bridge', *RCM Magazine*, XXXVII (1941).

'The Good Old Days', *RCM Magazine*, L (December 1954), 99.

'Frank Bridge', Dictionary of National Biography, 1941-50, L G Wickham Legg and E T Williams, eds. (Oxford University Press, 1959).

Keating, Roderick. 'The Songs of Frank Bridge' (University Microfilms, Ann Arbor, USA, 1970).

Lahee, H C. Annals of Music in America (Boston: Marshall Jones, 1922).

Lloyd Webber, Julian. 'The Cello Music of Frank Bridge', *The Strad* (April 1976).

Mitchell, Donald, and Hans Keller, eds. Benjamin Britten (Rockliff, 1952).

Musical Times, LXXXII (February 1941), 79 (unsigned obituary).

New York Times. Issues of November 6, 1938; February 23, 1941.

'E.N.' (Ernest Newman). *Sunday Times* (January 18, 1936).

Nolan, P J. *Musical America*, XXXIX (November 17, 1923), 3.

Payne, Anthony. 'Seeing Frank Bridge Whole'. *Daily Telegraph* (December 8, 1973).

'After a century of neglect', *Daily Telegraph* (December 2, 1972).

'Frank Bridge: the early years', *Tempo* 106 (September 1973).

'Frank Bridge: the last years', *Tempo* 107 (December 1973).

Sleeve-notes for Argo ZRG 714 (1973).

Sleeve-notes for HMV ALP 3190 (1976).

Sleeve-notes for Lyrita SRCS 91 (1976).

Pears, Peter. 'Frank Bridge', *Recorded Sound* (October 1976).

Pirie, Peter J. 'The Lost Generation', *Musical Times* (April 1955).

'Frank Bridge', *Musical Opinion*, LXXXVIII (June 1965), 531.

'The "Georgian" Composers', *The Listener* (August 12, 1965).

'The "Georgian" Composers', Music in Britain (The British Council, 1965).

'The Unfashionable Generation', *High Fidelity*, XVI (January 1966), 59.

'Debussy and English Music', *Musical Times*, CVIII (July 1967), 599.

'Frank Bridge' (Triad Press, 1971).

'Review of Pearl SHE 513/4, *Records and Recording* (August 1974).

Introduction to volume of four Bridge songs (Galliard, 1974).

'Frank Bridge's Piano Sonata', *Music and Musicians* (January 1976).

Rhodes, Harold. 'The R.C.M. of 50 Years Ago', *R.C.M. Magazine*, L (December 1954), 98.

Saerchinger, Cesar, ed. International Who's Who in Music, 1st ed. (New York: New York Current Literature, 1918).

Slonimsky, Nicholas, ed. Baker's Biographical Dictionary of Musicians, 5th ed. (New York: Schirmer, 1958).

Souster, Tim. 'Frank Bridge's Cello Sonata', *The Listener* (December 23, 1965).

The Times. Issues of September 25, 1913; November 6, 1915; October 16, 1916; October 31, 1918; October 8, 1920; March 10, 1921; November 18, 1921; October 27, 1936; January 13, 1941; January 17, 1941; January 30, 1961.

Variety, CXLI (Unsigned obituary. January 15, 1941), 54.

Walton, William. 'Modern Movement in Music', *School Music Review*, XXXIX (January, March and April 1929), 258, 326 and 366.

Warrack, John. 'A Note on Frank Bridge', *Tempo*, LXVI-LXVII (1963), 27.

Westrup, J A. *Daily Telegraph* (January 18, 1936).

'Frank Bridge', British Music of Our Time, ed. A L Bacharach (Pelican, 1946).

Whelbourn, Hubert. Celebrated Musicians Past and Present (Laurie, 1930).

Who's Who (New York: St. Martin's Press, all editions 1920-1940).

Who is Who in Music, 1941 edition (Chicago: Lee Stern, 1940).

Part of Bridge's own arrangement for cello and piano of his 'Oration'.

DISCOGRAPHY

JOHN BISHOP

Bridge as conductor made records in 1923-25 of music by Gounod, Humperdinck and Ravel, as well as of his own works *Sir Roger de Coverley*, the second of the *Two Poems* after Richard Jefferies, and *The Sea*. None of these are currently available, nor are the records he made as violist. However, there is some possibility that these may be reissued as an LP.

Full details of these records, as well as recordings of Bridge works by other artists, are contained in a comprehensive discography by Lewis Foreman, Eric Hughes and Malcolm Walker, to be published during 1976 in the BIRS magazine *Recorded Sound*.

The position about records of Bridge's music currently available (June 1976) is made the more complex by the imminent release of four LPs. Details of these are therefore included, probable release dates being:—

Lyrita	SRCS	91	September 1976
Decca	SDD	497	November 1976
Lyrita	SRCS	73	late 1976
Argo	ZRG	850	late 1976

In addition, the London Philharmonic Orchestra/Braithwaite have recorded the *Two Poems* after Richard Jefferies for Lyrita, for release in 1977, and there are provisional plans for recording *Oration, Rebus, Divertimenti*, the Rhapsody for 2 violins and viola (1928), and the Violin Sonata.

ORCHESTRAL

Cherry Ripe	Royal Liverpool Philharmonic/Groves	ASD 3190
	London Philharmonic/Boult	SRCS 73
Enter Spring	Royal Liverpool Philharmonic/Groves	ASD 3190
Lament	Royal Liverpool Philharmonic/Groves	ASD 3190
Rosemary	London Philharmonic/Boult	SRCS 73
Sally in Our Alley	London Philharmonic/Boult	SRCS 73
(The) Sea	Royal Liverpool Philharmonic/Groves	ASD 3190
Suite for strings	London Philharmonic/Boult	SRCS 73
Sir Roger de Coverley	London Philharmonic/Boult	SRCS 73
	English Chamber/Britten	SXL 6405
Summer	Royal Liverpool Philharmonic/Groves	ASD 3190
There is a Willow Grows Aslant a Brook	English Sinfonia/Dilkes	CSD 3696

Phantasm	London Philharmonic/Braithwaite, Wallfisch	SRCS 91

CHAMBER

[Three] Noveletten	Gabrielli String Quartet	SDD 497
[Three] Idylls	Gabrielli String Quartet	SDD 497
Piano Trio No.2	Tunnell Trio	ZRG 850
Phantasy Piano Quartet	Tunnell Trio/Brian Hawkins	ZRG 850
Sonata for Cello and Piano	Rostropovitch/Britten	SXL 6426
String Quartet No.3	Allegri Quartet	ZRG 714
String Quartet No.4	Allegri Quartet	ZRG 714

ORGAN

Adagio in E	Preston	ZRG 528
	Herrick	VPS 1001
Allegro Marziale (Organ Pieces, book 1)	Dearnley	CSD 3677

PIANO

(The) Hour Glass (Three Pieces)	Wallfisch	SHE 513/4
Rosemary	Moore	Saga 5400
Solitude (Three Poems)	Wallfisch	SHE 513/4
Sonata	Wallfisch	SHE 513/4
Through the Eaves (In Autumn)	Wallfisch	SHE 513/4
Winter Pastoral	Wallfisch	SHE 513/4

SONGS

Blow Out, You Bugles	Johnston/Hinden	SHE 513/4
Come to Me in My Dreams	Baulard/Vignoles	SHE 513/4
Day after Day	Baulard/Vignoles	SHE 513/4
Dweller in My Deathless Dreams	Johnston/Hinden	SHE 513/4
Go Not, Happy Day	Pears/Britten	ECS 545
	Baulard/Vignoles	SHE 513/4

Goldenhair	Pears/Britten	ZRG 5418
Journey's End	Pears/Britten	ZRG 5418
	Baulard/Vignoles	SHE 513/4
[The] Last Invocation	Baulard/Hinden	SHE 513/4
Love Went A-riding	Pears/Britten	ECS 545
	Johnston/Hinden	SHE 513/4
Mantel of Blue	Baulard/Hinden	SHE 513/4
So Perverse	Pears/Britten	ZRG 5418
	Johnston/Hinden	SHE 513/4
Strew No More Red Roses	Johnston/Hinden	SHE 513/4
	Pears/Britten	ZRG 5418
'Tis but a Week	Johnston/Hinden	SHE 513/4
What Shall I Your True Love Tell?	Baulard/Vignoles	SHE 513/4
When You Are Old	Pears/Britten	ZRG 5418
Where She Lies Asleep	Johnston/Hinden	SHE 513/4

INDEX

to the Bridge works listed in Anthony Payne's section (pages 9-51). Works whose title begins with 'A' or 'The' are listed under the second word of the title.

April, 28

Bittersweet, 28

Cello Sonata, 10, 21, 25, 27, 28, 31, 32
Christmas Rose, The, 27
Columbine, 28

Dainty Rogue, 28
Dance Poem, 17, 19, 21, 28, 30
Dance Rhapsody, 17, 19
Day After Day, 30
Dedication, A, 29
Dew Fairy, The, 29
Divertimenti, 43, 45
Dweller in My Deathless Dreams, 30

Enter Spring, 23, 36, 38, 46

Fairy Tale, A, 28
Fireflies, 28
Four Characteristic Pieces, 28

Go Not, Happy Day, 29
Graziella, 29

Heart's Ease, 28
Hedgerow, The, 28
Hour Glass, The, 28, 29

Idylls, 13
In Autumn, 29
Into Her Keeping, 30

Last Invocation, The, 30
Love Went A-Riding, 29

Midnight Tide, The, 29
Miniature Pastorals, 28

Novelletten, 13

Oration, 45, 48, 49

Phantasie Trio, 10, 11, 13, 25, 41
Phantasm, 46, 47, 48, 49
Phantasy Quartet, 10, 11, 13, 15, 24, 25
Piano Sonata, 27, 28, 29, 30
Piano Trio (2nd), 38, 39
Piano Quartet, 10
Piano Quintet, 11, 15, 25
Prayer, A, 25

Rebus, 45, 46, 51
Retrospect, 29
Revel, A, 28
Rhapsody Trio, 11, 38, 39, 43
Rosemary, 28

Sea, The, 15
Solitude, 28, 30
So Perverse, 29
Speak To Me, My Love, 30
Strew No More Red Roses, 30
String Sextet, 15
String Quintet — 1st, 13, 15
———— 2nd, 21, 24, 27
———— 3rd, 30, 32, 35, 36, 38, 39, 43
———— 4th, 11, 43, 44, 49, 51
Summer, 21, 24, 30
Sunset, 28

There is A Willow Grows Aslant a Brook, 35, 36, 38
Three Improvisations, 28
Three Lyrics, 28
Three Pieces, 28
Three Poems, 28

Three Sketches, 28
Through the Eaves, 29
Thy Hand in Mine, 30
'Tis But a Week, 30
Two Poems, 21, 22, 24, 28

Valse Capricieuse, 28

Violin Sonata, 38, 43

What Shall I Your True Love Tell?, 30
Where She Lies Asleep, 29
When You Are Old, 30
Winter Pastoral, 29